191

CHRISTIAN FAITH SERIES

Reinhold Niebuhr, CONSULTING EDITOR

Love Almighty and Ills Unlimited

BY AUSTIN FARRER

Love Almighty

and

Ills Unlimited

AN ESSAY ON PROVIDENCE AND EVIL

CONTAINING THE NATHANIEL TAYLOR LECTURES FOR 1961

Marsden

BY AUSTIN FARRER

WARDEN OF KEBLE COLLEGE, OXFORD

Doubleday & Company, Inc.

Garden City, New York 1961

Library of Congress Catalog Card Number 61–8883
Copyright © 1961 by Austin Farrer
All Rights Reserved. Printed in the United States of America
First Edition

Contents

Love Almighty and Ills Unlimited

The Question

Evil commonly strikes us not as a problem, but as an outrage. Taken in the grip of misfortune, or appalled by the violence of malice, we cannot reason sanely about the balance of the world. Indeed, it is part of the problem of evil that its victim is rendered incapable of thought. So, if we are to start with the sufferer, there are two problems, the first practical, the second theoretical. First, he must recover the power of dispassionate vision; and second, he must exercise it on the place held by evil, including his own trouble, in the whole scheme of things. The practical problem is pastoral, medical, or psychological, and differs from case to case too widely to allow of much useful generalization. We are concerned with the theoretical problem only. If what we say is neither comforting nor tactful, we need not mind. Our business is to say, if we can, what is true. So far from beginning with the sufferer and his personal distresses, we will attempt to get the issue into perspective, and sketch the widest possible view.

The evil in our life is an obstacle to belief, and a thorn in the Christian's side; but in one of his sides only. It is not every aspect of our faith, nor every article of our creed, to which the mixture of evil and good is an embarrassment. It troubles us, certainly, when we try to understand the ways of a fatherly Providence; so many things happen which look anything rather than providential. But suppose we shift our ground, and attend to a point of doctrine even more fundamental, perhaps, than providence. The thoughtful Christian looks at the world, and wonders why he ever dreamt of looking beyond it; why he ever supposed it to require a cause outside itself, an origin transcendent or divine. What reasons incline a man to acknowledge a creative Power? What but the mixture of good and evil? Here is the springboard of theistic argument. Everyone must surely see that a world like ours is the battleground of good, but neither its home nor its origin. Here splendors are displayed dazzlingly bright, but astonishingly brittle and precarious. Have they nowhere a hold on reality more solid and more sure? Are they not rooted in an eternity behind the world? If our universe were the safe abode of its own highest glories, if its noblest constituents were secure from the evils which everywhere attack and corrupt them, the world might be God enough to itself; being what it is, it depends on God above it.

Such a line of persuasion is nothing more than a special development of the classic argument from our world to God. The liability of everything we value to suffer adulteration and decay is simply an aspect of that "contingency," that subjection to accident, that brutal irrationality of occurrence, which traditional philosophy has made the hallmark of a finite being, dependent on Infinite God for its existence.

A traditional philosopher might carry the argument still further. He might claim, not only that the world's imperfections suggest God's existence, but that they define the very meaning of his Name. Just as "light" means nothing to us except as the opposite of "darkness," so "God" has no sense in our ears except by way of contrast with "world." And what is the difference between them? Is it not precisely this, that God is a being single and unmixed, a goodness absolute, whereas the world is a confusion of activities in mutual strife, their existence continually at stake, their good always unsure, their ills often inescapable?

Light and dark are pure and simple opposites, both unmixed; and such is also, perhaps, the opposition between good and evil. "God" and "world" are not opposed like this, an unmixed negative against an unmixed positive. The contrast lies in the mixed nature of one, and the unmixed character of the other. God is a simple goodness; the world's good is mixed with many faults and flaws.

We must concede, as a point of mere theory, that the imperfection of things need not go to such a length as we see it do, for there to be a difference between creation and its creator. A harmonious society of archangels would already fall an infinite distance below the perfection of God, and the mind of an archangel would be quick to acknowledge the interval. But we are not archangels. Our minds are scaled to the world of which we form a part, and require the violent sort of evidence which it supplies. The more outrageous the mixture, the more preposterous the tragicomedy of good and evil, the more striking for us the evidence of deity. Is not this universe of ours, of all possible worlds, the most plainly dependent on a higher Goodness? What other could so loudly call for the recognition of its creator and sustainer? Our realm of values is riddled with holes. Will it float for a moment, unsustained by the invisible almighty hand?

The argument we have outlined is no fabrication of ours; it is in substance traditionally Christian. Christian difficulties over good and evil do not arise until a fresh step is taken. Having satisfied our minds about the existence of a Creator, we stop asking whether the world was made, and ask why it should have been made as it is. The painful riddle is immediately posed: why should an omnipotent Goodness desire to frame a world like this? Or why, supposing him to have framed it, does he not govern it better? If God is light, and in him no darkness at all, surely he loves the glories, and hates the shadows of any world he forms. And must not the glories which delight him flourish, the shadows he detests decay? So reason would suggest, but it is not so that experience teaches. Since the day when Satan tempted Job, calling God's providence in doubt by ruining his faithful servant, Job's question has been with us; and it would be a bold man who claimed it had been answered.

To Christians, then, the mixed character of the world is not so much an honest enemy as a treacherous ally, changing sides in the heat of the battle. It supports us in our proof of a Creator, but turns against our endeavour to understand him. A philosophical critic has an easy opening here. The moral of our absurd predicament, he will say, is that we have advanced on to false ground. We ought never to have raised the question which proves our intellectual torment. God's purposes in creating or in directing the world are past our finding out; if, indeed, they ought to be called "purposes" at all. The mystery of creation is ultimate. God threw this universe into being, and the exploration of its marvels will exhaust our faculties. Why he has formed it as he has, why made it a war of atoms rather than, let us say, a choir of angels, is not the sort of question we can meaningfully ask. The interplay of the world's constituents produces what we are pleased to call its goods and evils. The world being so constituted, such will its goods and evils be.

So says our philosophical critic, and adds, perhaps, with a smile: "But you are not content to let it go at that. You want religion. If so, no doubt you will have to venture further; and do the best you can with the logical agonies in which you will involve yourselves." Shall we agree to such a division of the credit between us—that we may be pious, but that he is wise? No, we shall claim to be the wiser in truth, and the more philosophical. Belief in God, we shall maintain, is essentially a practical and a passionate belief. A true philosophy of human nature will itself persuade us that man is not an animal either so passionless or so theoretical as to achieve an abstract conviction of God's existence apart from any active relation to his will. It would be a belief, at the best, for philosophers. But this is to say that it would not even be a belief. For no man is a philosopher when it comes to believing. Philosophy does not create belief, it tests or systematizes it.

Theoretically considered, a perception of the world's insufficiency or faultiness justifies the conjecture of an all-sufficient Creator. But in personal fact, we experience imperfection and precariousness in ourselves, not in the objects of our detached contemplation. We turn to God not as an explanatory cause, but as a saving power; not as the ground of all existence, but as a rock on which to plant our feet; or rather, as himself our rescuer from that whirlpool, in which all things, whether good or evil, senseless or sentient, are sucked down.

Philosophy herself will be wise to admit that our evidence
for God is always the evidence of his activity, and most forcible
where it touches us nearest. And where is that? No doubt
the activity of the Creator comes home to us when divine
eternity is felt through the veil of perishable things. Yet men
have never, in the mass, felt the Maker in his works, without
at the same time finding their wills engaged with the action
of a Savior. There are, indeed, religions which strike us as
purely naturalistic; as identifying the Divine with creative
force alone, or with the very nerve and marrow of nature's
being. But such a faith is as practical as any other. Its aim is
not a selfless contemplation of natural fact. In identifying
nature with God, it teaches that the springs of life are wholesome. It holds us out the hope that we may somehow wrap our
roots round the fountain of existence, drinking up the nourishment of our good, or invigorating our struggle against besetting harms. Religious naturalism may conceal, but cannot
eliminate the saving function of the godhead. What religion
ever was the indifferent submission to a Maker and Breaker
of souls? A theology which stops short at creation, and dis-
interests itself in the conflict of evil with the divine goodness,
handles a one-sided abstraction, which is not even the diagram of an actual belief.

Not every religion is so undisguisedly paradoxical as the
Christian; not every religion sees the beneficent action of the
divine power as that of a fatherly providence. Yet to the
Christian at least his religion will seem for this very reason
most religious, most open and genuine; it carries faith in the
saving action of God to the furthest point, and lives in that
strange appeal from God to God, which no religion can wholly
escape. God has made the world, but he has made it (for our

purposes) so cruelly, that we appeal to Him, to save us from its evils. We cannot appeal to any other, or suppose two Gods, one who makes, and one who redeems us; none but the author of nature can have that mastery of things, which enables Him to save to the uttermost. The Rock on which we hope to stand is the ground and principle of all being. Were He anything less than this, he would be threatened by the transience of created things and could provide us no ultimate refuge. But then again—and here is the paradox—if the God who saves us is the author of nature, then the evil from which he saves us is part and parcel of the nature he has made. The last enemy he vanquishes for us is death; yet death is his appointment; for what is more natural than to die? When we appeal to the God of nature, is it not against the God of nature that we make our appeal?

Once this point has been seized, it is an easy matter to tighten the cords of argument, and torture the paradox. If Omnipotence (we may ask) will indeed save us, why does he first permit the ruin from which he later grants the rescue? What should we think of a man who, to gratify a capricious philanthropy, allowed the prevalence of evils he was able to prevent? Who multiplied victims, that he might pick beneficiaries? Perhaps he will confer benefits on everyone, and make us all happy in the end. But even so, how is he to justify our foregoing miseries?

If we talk in such a strain, and work up the paradox, it is not so that we may glory in it, or even that we may prove it insoluble. We mean to go as far towards a solution as we can; but meanwhile we sharpen our apprehension of the problem we propose to solve, for fear we should let ourselves off too lightly. As to the attitude which revels in paradox,

theologians have been known to indulge it, but it is unworthy
of a rational creature, all the same. It is always our duty to
find as much sense and order in things as we can. Acquiescence
in the paradox of existence, or appeal to the unintelligibility
of things divine, is justifiable only as a last resort.

Anyone who attempts a philosophy of providence and
evil is sure to have Job's comforters brandished in his face.
Job's comforters, we know, merited divine rebuke; not, however, because they reasoned, but because they lied. Either,
they said, our troubles do us good, or they are the just penalty
of our faults. Job perceived that the innocent suffer no less
than the guilty; a later generation has discovered that trouble
injures more souls than it benefits. Trouble is, indeed, the acid
test of virtue; but only because its tendency is to destroy it.
In the same way, a pestilent climate is the test of health.
We have no need to go to the opposite extreme, and make
the lap of luxury the nursery of character. A little hardness
may be all to the good; but frustration and misery rot the
soul away.

Job's comforters are liars; and their mendacity is a moral
fault, not simply a speculative failure. It is the hardness of a
heart which refuses to feel the sorrow it dares to explain.
Eliphaz and Zophar close their eyes upon the fact which it is
their boast to interpret; and in forcing the case for God's
compassion, they destroy their own capacity for pity. In
justifying Providence they come near to justifying evil; and
evil can never be justified; it is theologically defined as what
God himself detests. Some evils, indeed, are evils in appearance
only; evils in our eyes, not in the eyes of God. But to pretend
that all evils are merely apparent is the cruellest and most
revolting of paradoxes. Mary Baker Eddy went to the limit

in denying the reality of evil; yet even her deity is left with something to hate and to destroy—that mortal error which creates all the harms it falsely supposes.

Through faults both of intellect and character, Job's comforters mismanage their task; but it is a proper enough task in itself. It is useless, after all, to pretend that God's ways and purposes are an open book to everyone. If they perplex us, we shall discuss them with our friends, and hope to understand better by talking together. So Job speaks, and his companions answer. The sufferer accuses God; and is not the believer to defend him? Not, of course, in the spirit of an advocate defending a client. For the client is supposed incapable of his own defense; the lawyer's business is to make a case for him. But God is a living, self-justifying truth, and to plead for him can only be to say what he says, to capture an echo of his meaning in the idioms of our stammering speech. If we are prophets, we can utter what he newly speaks through us; if theologians, what he signifies by old revelation; if philosophers, what he has expressed in his created works. For our part we will not claim to prophesy. Whether what we endeavor to write is philosophy or theology, there is no need beforehand to decide. In either case, none of it will be our own. There is nothing new to say on the subject. Only the fashions of speech alter, and ancient argument is freshly phrased.

Job complains of his own malady. If all the ways of God were just beside, still God has been unjust to him. But no— looking further afield, he sees all too much evidence that his own case is typical. So the riddle of evil is felt in a single case, and afterwards generalized. But a discussion like ours will commonly start on the level of generalization. We take up the complaint that the world is bad, or not nearly good

enough; or that God has mixed into its constitution an intolerable surplus of unnecessary evils.

A monstrous generalization, like a staggering lie, may sometimes pass, where a more restricted claim would be challenged.
The vast assertion, the mighty lie, overwhelms our faculties,
and puts our art of criticism out of action. If someone said
to us that the rising generation is more stupid than the last,
we should immediately protest at so fantastic a generality.
We should not admit that there was anything that could be
seriously discussed—let alone conceded—until the statement
had been broken down into smaller parts. What sort, or sorts
of stupidity, had the speaker in mind? Are his young acquaint-
ances lacking in personal understanding, or in technical ability? Is the general level of competence low, or is there less
exceptional brilliance, less erratic fire? Are they ill-educated,
or are they uneducable? Are they slow-witted, or are they
glibly proficient? Stupidity is too general a complaint, and a
generation is too wide a class to accuse of it. But now let us
broaden the generalization many million times in both directions. Stupidity is only one sort of evil; let us talk of all the
evil there is. The young English or Americans are a limited
class in one animal species; let us indict the Universe. And
with what result? Are we greeted with exasperated derision?
No, we are felt to have struck a level philosophical and profound; we have raised the pure issue, the issue of evil as such.

"Never mind," says the accommodating skeptic, with a
shrug of the shoulders; "I will not take you back over the steps
which led you to your enormous generality. I will pick you
up where I find you. You have made a general accusation:
there is more evil of every sort in the world than a good
Creator would introduce, or a kind Providence could tolerate.

Well now, I might take the line that evil is a hopelessly vague word, for which no single value can be fixed. But I will not. I will be candid enough to admit that 'evil' has a single sense throughout. But that sense is subjective. Many classes of conditions are universally bad—say physical conditions disturbing to the pattern of animal life. But by calling something bad, we do not mean that it belongs to any such single class. All disease is bad, but not all badness is disease; and when we call disease itself bad, we are not just saying that disease is disease; we are saying that it is to be deplored—deplored, that is, by a sound judgement. The only sense of 'evil' which will cover all cases is just this. To what, then, does your indictment of the Universe amount? To the statement that it contains more deplorable things than divine goodness would tolerate.

"But now," our critic continues, "*deplorable* is a subjective term. You may say, 'No; the things you complain of *ought* to be deplored.' But how can you be sure of that? All you can ever show is that they are such as to be deplored in fact by you and your friends; and that by describing them to us, you can make us equally deplore them. But when you say that their deplorability unbalances the universe, and shows almighty wisdom failing effectively to deplore what ought to be deplored, surely you go too far. Who is more likely to deplore the right things, God or you?"

"Ah," we reply, "that sounds well enough in theory; and where variety of judgment is possible, no doubt God's mind holds a balance more delicate than ours. But it is nonsense, it is blasphemy to suggest that any mind, let alone the divine, can approve the ravages of cancer or the cruelties of Hitler, starved bellies in the East or starved affections in the West."

"Very well," our critic rejoins, "and I heartily concur. But now you have descended once more from the general to the particular. You have stopped talking about evil on the whole, and begun to specify typically bad things. This is how I should myself wish to see the question approached. Only, if we are to make any progress with it, we shall need more system, and less rhetoric. It is not enough to cite telling examples. We must divide evils into several sorts by some rational principle of division; and then we must try to see how each sort may be related to a divine will."

It is difficult for us to disagree with our critic, or to shirk the task he proposes to us. We should like to go straight to the discussion of those evils which are most heartbreaking, most unmerited, and most utterly useless in the world. But if we are properly to judge the bearing of them when we reach them, we must proceed more patiently, and more philosophically; we must first attempt some more general account of things good and evil. We shall, in fact, find ourselves driven to save the burning cases for the latest treatment; we shall clear out of the way the easiest examples first, and advance through progressive degrees of cruciality.

CHAPTER II

Dualist Heresy

Any discussion of goods and evils must begin with the great platitude established by the Fathers of the Church in opposition to the dualistic heretics, and especially by St. Augustine against the Manichees.

"Evil" in general, we have said, is that which we find ourselves obliged to deplore. In the same way "good" is what we cannot help approving. So there are laudable things, and there are deplorable things; and the heretics assigned them to two different sources, two creative powers almost on a level with one another. They thought that the world was a mosaic of goods and evils, as a mosaic pavement may be composed of black and white marble squares. It would be reasonable enough to suppose that the blacks and whites had come from different quarries; and so the heretics derived goods and evils from different creators. It worried them that the two had ever got mixed together. An arrangement of black and white marble may be a happy design, but a mixture of goods and evils is not. If only we could take it to pieces, and put the two colors of existence each back into the quarry from which each originally came!

The Fathers pointed out the absurdity of such a picture: the things in the world which we deplore are not to be compared with black squares in a mosaic, but with flawed squares. Some of the marble blocks always had a poor grain and color; others of them have split or crumbled. Good pieces and bad pieces come all from the same quarry—at least there is no reason why they should not. They are not different sorts; they are perfect and defective examples of the same sort. A bad man is not a devil; he is a warped specimen of mankind, and it is this very fact that makes him so distressing to contemplate. Disease is not its own way of being; it is the breakdown of health. Evil is essentially the parasite of a good, whose existence it presupposes.

It is often said that the dependence works equally both ways—just as evil is evil by attacking good, so good is good by triumphing over evil. For "good" and "bad" are terms of mutual contrast; if nothing were bad, we should not bother to call anything good. Neither should we bother to call anything bright, if nothing were dark. But the argument is a fallacy; it confuses things with our awareness of them. The imaginary man on a desert island alone might never have met with or heard of disease. He has never been ill himself; and he would not know what it meant to tell himself that he is well today. But this morning, going down to the familiar shore to look for turtles' eggs, he meets an unfamiliar sight—a shipwrecked sailor, half-starved, half-drowned, and desperately ill. By contrast with the stranger's condition, our Crusoe becomes conscious of his own good health. But what he becomes conscious of is something he had all the time, and quite independently of the stranger's arrival. His consciousness of health is new; the health of which he is conscious is old; it is the (uninhibited) functioning of his bodily system; and disease is no ingredient in it.

But now let us take the opposite case. A monotonous diet of turtles' eggs from speechless infancy has not agreed with our poor Crusoe's stomach. Alas, he has never been well; he has led but half a life, crawling pitifully and with pain about his island. His condition, however miserable, has been stable. He has not had noticeably worse and better days. And so it would mean nothing for him to tell himself that he is ill this morning—this morning, which is to bring him so great a surprise. For, from a freshly beached canoe a gleaming, grinning savage comes bounding up the shore; and by contrast with this splendid vision, poor Crusoe comes to recognize the sickness of his own condition. Though he never knew it till now, he has always been wretchedly ill. It takes a healthy man to show him this. He always knew that he could not run like the wild goats any more than he could fly like the pigeons of his island. If he could, he would have enjoyed a more varied diet. But it never struck him that he could, or should in any sense, have been a pigeon or a goat; nor that there were pigeon-powers or goat-powers within him, spoiled and inhibited. No, goats and pigeons were just different. But what he now sees is that he should have been a man. He has in himself an animal constitution which has been frustrated, and prevented by circumstance from being itself. Unless human health had always been in some sense an unrealized possibility he would have been not a sick man, but an inferior creature—a unique example of the Crusoe species, and simply different. Disease, we formerly said, is not an ingredient in health; but health, we now see, is always an ingredient in disease—or rather, not an ingredient in it, but the subject of it. Health is what gets diseased; or the misfunctioning of health is that wherein disease consists.

So then, said the Fathers to the heretics, there are not two sorts of things, good things and bad things, somehow scrambled together in a universe. There are many sorts of things, and each sort, if given its head and allowed to be itself, is good; if warped, spoiled, or inhibited, it is bad. It follows that you cannot accuse God, or the devil either, of creating evil beings. You can accuse God—let us hope unjustly—of neglect, in allowing things created good in kind, to prove failures. Or you can accuse the devil, if you believe in him, of breaking into God's paradise, and spoiling his creations. Such accusations may be unfounded, but at least they make sense. The accusation of creating bad sorts cannot even be discussed, for it means nothing: "bad sort" being a contradiction in terms.

"But that's absurd," exclaims my neighbor, who spends half his life in his garden. What is the use of denying that you can have bad sorts? I've a bad sort of strawberries in this bed, and I mean to get rid of them. There are many better sorts to be had."

"You are quite right," I answer. "Of course we used the expression *bad sort* in cases like this, and very sensibly too. When I said *bad sort* was a nonsensical phrase, I must have been using *sort* in a rather special way. What was I talking about? Was it not about sorts of things which God might be said to have appointed, or made? Such as strawberries, for example? But now along come the clever gardeners, and breed a special strain of strawberry which they think is going to be better than any other; but they are not as clever as they suppose, and in fact it proves the reverse. Their new strain turns out to be very bad at being a strawberry—it gets all the diseases there are and its fruit molders at the least touch of damp. A bad sort, we say; and similarly we may have bad sorts of men—bullies, for instance, or hypocrites. But all the time we are taking for granted the goodness of a sort of being —in the one case strawberries, in the other case men. For unless it was a good thing to be a strawberry, or a human being, we should not complain that certain sorts of either kind were bad at it."

My gardening friend is still unconvinced. "Look at that," he says, pulling up a long trail of fleshy white root, carrying rank green shoots. "That's not a gardener's fancy, nor a bad specimen of its kind, either. That's ground elder, that is, and God made it, and every gardener knows it's a wicked sort— in fact, it's a pestilent weed."

"Don't I know it," I reply. "It comes all under the fence from you to me. But when we call it bad, we mean it's bad for us, or for the plants we are trying to grow. It's a fine, flourishing thing in itself, and we'd be glad to think of it filling waste land, if it would only keep out of our way. Things do get across one another in this world, it cannot be denied, and then one is bad for the other. When that happens, there is once more a goodness presupposed—not the goodness of the thing which does the harm, but the goodness of the thing which suffers it. If we say the ground elder is bad for the strawberries, we are not suggesting that the ground elder is capable of good behavior but is, in the present case, behaving badly. We are assuming that the strawberries could be their own excellent selves, but that the ground elder hinders them."

"That goes for wasps, too, I take it," says my friend. "They are fine enough creatures, when you come to think of it, and I've no complaints against their home life; it just is that their ideas and ours happen to conflict. But what about these spiders I was reading of? They're not nice, whatever way you look at them, especially the females. Some of them eat their young, as soon as they're hatched, if they don't get away quick enough; and others of them eat their mate, as soon as he's paired with them. And that's nature; it's the way they were made to be."

"It doesn't sound pretty, one has to admit," I reply. "But when we complain of such goings on, it's a puzzle what we mean. We seem to be saying that such conduct doesn't come up to standard—the spiders are deviationists. But from what? Not from the standard of their own species, evidently; for this is how the species behaves. It is not ladylike; but why expect spiders to be ladies? To say that they ought to love their off-spring or their mates is surely nonsense. Insects may be capable of pleasure; they are not capable of love. We do not expect them to go against the preservation of their own kind, or anyhow their own branch of it. But in fact the spiders do not. The ordeal of the offspring—run, or mother will eat you—im-proves the strain by eliminating the unfit; and the killing of the father so that he only acts once probably has the same effect. The business of the father is paternity. He can do noth-ing more for his children, once he has begotten them, except to feed the womb that carries them; and this he does, by getting eaten. What then do we mean by our revulsion? We do not expect spiders to have the manners of ladies, or even the morals of Hottentots. But we have got used to observing some degree of analogy between the family ethics of mankind and the instinctive behavior of brute creatures; and when the analogy breaks down so shockingly, ·we feel a moral disgust.

"There is no need for the present to decide whether we are wise to deplore the spider. It will be enough, if we can see what it would mean, to do so. And the way it looks is this: we should be assuming an idea of what a living creature is like. It need not be human, but it must, as it were, be tending in the human direction, anyhow in certain ways. The spider deviates. If we are evolutionists, we may say that the species has developed unhappily in a wrong direction. Just as 'music' allows of very different developments, and yet must always be faithful to certain basic principles, so (we must be taken to suppose) it will be with the living creatures. Some music is bad music, because it is out of line; and so some living creatures are bad, and spiders are like this. If we treated our spiders on their own merits, as examples of their own sort, we should be powerless to criticize them. If we criticize them, we are (whether we know it or not) treating them as constituting one variety of a more basic sort, living creature, from which they have deviated, or fallen away. They may have fallen from being innocent, or humane spiders. They may have fallen into being spiders, from being creatures of a more innocent sort. In either case the principle of St. Augustine is saved; if anything is bad in itself (and not merely bad for some other thing), it is 'a bad so-and-so,' and this so-and-so, or sort, cannot itself be bad. (Burglars are bad, and John Smith is a bad, i.e., an incompetent, burglar; but to say so is not to express a genuine condemnation. To be bad at being bad is not to be bad absolutely. A man who says, 'I am terribly bad at keeping up a quarrel' is praising himself, and knows it.)"

While I am prosing away in this strain, and riding my philosophical hobby, my gardening neighbor takes up his fork, and returns to the attack on his old enemy, the ground elder. With a sudden grunt, he rears up, and lays his hand on his loins. "Lumbago," he says. "And what about that? Are you going to say that it's good in itself, and only bad for me? Or that it's bad in itself by failing to be a really good pain? It's quite good enough at being a pain, if you ask me. I should say it's a thorough bad thing."

"Thoroughly bad," I reply, "but not a thing. On the packet of Dr. Sidebottom's Lumbago Powder, the disease is represented as a somewhat scraggy little dragon, biting a sufferer in the part affected; while Dr. Sidebottom (if he is the figure with the high collar and the luxuriant mustaches) pitches into the aggressor with an outsize toasting fork. But all this, we know, is allegory. If lumbago were really a dragon, it might be like the wasps we were speaking of—good at being a dragon, but bad for you; while Dr. Sidebottom, if we have to believe him, would, in turn, be bad for it. But your lumbago is not a dragon— it is only you, or a bit of you, misfunctioning and hurting. To call it bad is to say that it would be good for you neither to hurt nor to misfunction in this way, but to enjoy what you optimistically call your usual health."

My friend, defeated by lumbago if not by argument, abandons the garden, and the discussion. I go my own way, convinced, as usual, by my own voice. Nothing is called bad but by reference to the spoiling of a nature, the inhibition of an activity, the frustration of an aim, or the saddening of a existence which we take to be good. St. Augustine was perfectly right; indeed, as we said at our first mention of him, platitudinously so; and we may wonder why he was felt to have made so great a point against the heretics. You have not made the world out any better, in saying it is spoilt by its own anarchy and decay, rather than by adulteration with a dark element, foreign to its nature. If the milkman brings us curdled milk, we may not greatly care whether he has dropped acid into it, or simply let it turn bad; either way it is undrinkable. St. Augustine has not eased the problem of evil, or exculpated God. He has merely defended the single origin of the world. A good God created good sorts. The problem remains, why he should let them go so rotten.

Nevertheless, St. Augustine's platitude lays down a line for further investigation to follow. We had ourselves decided that the problem of evil was far too general in its absolute statement, to allow of immediate discussion. We must break it up into parts. We must relate evils, not evil, to the will of God; and since we cannot take all particular evils one by one, we want a rational principle, to divide them into kinds. Now St. Augustine has given us such a principle. For evil, he says, is the spoiling of some created thing; and if so, there are likely to be as many broad classes of evil as there are broad classes of things created. "Animal, vegetable, or mineral?" ask the children in their old guessing game. We must consider animal, vegetable, and mineral evil—or if that is not quite the division we require, let us hope to find a list not greatly more complicated.

CHAPTER III

The Potter and the Clay

"Animal, vegetable, or mineral," like so much nursery wisdom, is pre-evolutionary. It begins from the top of the scale, and our first move will be to turn it the other way round. We will take things in the order in which we suppose them to have come, and make a start with lifeless nature.

In all the thousand million years when there was a universe, and nothing lived, what are we to say of its good, or what of its evil? What would be a bad thing, in those days? Suppose a star exploded. You might say it was bad. But bad for what? For the star? Is the suggestion anything better than the fanciful personification of a molten mass? Can a star be receptive of good or evil? Perhaps we go too far, indeed, if we limit to persons the liability to suffer damage. Let us agree that any vital unit may. The least developed of animals will have a life cycle proper to its kind; and if it is cut off before the cycle is completed, it has failed to be all itself, or to execute its whole function. If a young snail is crushed, the damage to the sum of things is small. If it had lived, it would have spoiled several handsome plants; and by its death it feeds a songbird. Nevertheless a price is paid for these advantages: the destruction of an individual creature. But what is destroyed when a star explodes? And what, to begin with, is a star? A cohesive mass of molten rocks. If they are scattered, has anything perished? Suppose I rake out the fire and scatter the embers. Who is to weep for a being called "the fire," formerly made up of these parts, but now cruelly sundered and slain? While I still wanted to sit up, the fire was a boon to me, and I could easily personify an object for my gratitude: a cheerful spirit, the Vesta of the hearth, twisting her flames in a lively dance. But the unitary being of the fire would be in my imagination, and the good of it would be mine, not its own. Whereas we are thinking of a time before the fanciful brain, or sentient nerve, when stars were not yet rushlights for distant men. If they exploded and scattered, there was a different arrangement of material energy; and that was all.

"Very well," someone may admit, "let a star be an assembly of particles, as a rainbow is of falling drops; less transient, indeed, than the rainbow, but no more genuine a unit; no more capable of actualizing good, or of enduring evil. But what if we view the bursting star as the member of a stellar system? As contributory to such systems, the formation of stars must surely seem progressive, and their destruction correspondingly retrograde. Suppose (to take the negative extreme) matter remained uniformly scattered over space, as a featureless ocean of rarefied gas. Then, though something indeed would exist, you could scarcely call it a world. But if matter clots into masses and these arrange themselves in galaxies, or perhaps, on a smaller scale, in solar systems like our own, creation is surely proceeding apace. Whereas if there are no stars, no masses, there can be no such systems. If all stars exploded, the stellar universe would be dis-created. Should we not say, then, that the explosion of any star must impoverish, so far as it goes, the system to which that star belongs? That it is dis-creative, and therefore evil?"

Evil, yes, perhaps, but whose evil? If a star is not a unitary enough being to have evil or good pinned upon it, how much less so is a universe, or a galaxy, or any other such enormous sprawl of floating parts! Shall we then be driven to locate the evil in the disappointment of a cosmic engineer, who sees his great machine undergo a partial breakdown? That will scarcely do, for the universe is not a machine, nor is God an engineer. Machines are man-made things, and when men make them, they impose upon certain parts of God's handiwork a fixity of order which he had not imparted. The world-machine was discredited three centuries ago. Our museums contain ingenious toys made in brass, armillary spheres and orreries, supposed by a former age truly to represent the pattern and movement of the universe. As the astrologer constructed his concentric rings of brass, so God had ordered his crystalline spheres, arranging them to revolve one outside another, at fixed ratios of distance, speed, and angle. Each carried its luminary, set in it like a jewel; only the outermost sphere was encrusted with whole arabesques of constellated fire. On such a view, the world was a machine, the *alta mundi machina;* and the explosion of a star would represent a mechanical fault, like the breaking of a wheel. But it was not going to happen; the world-machine was perfect, and accident unthinkable. If, to suppose the preposterous, it should occur, it must disappoint the omnipotent designer. Or, since the thought of his disappointment was doubly and trebly preposterous, we should have to suppose that the apparent accident was his intention. He had never meant his world to endure forever; it was to perish on the Day of Wrath. If he broke a detail of his masterpiece beforehand, he meant it as a warning and a sign to scorners of the coming Judgment.

There is no need to labor the point that the world we know is not that of the Christian or Arabian Aristotelist. But it is still possible for us dumbly to feel that though the world is not like that, it ought to be; that its failure to achieve the perfection of mechanical design disappoints the full intention of its Creator. If the galaxies cannot be as neat as Aristotle's spheres they ought at least to reach the tidiness of the diagram in which the modern student sketches to himself their general aspect. Since they do not, we may feel, so much the worse for them; or rather, since "they" are not possible objects of our commiseration, so much the worse for their Creator's design.

What we have just written is perhaps a caricature. None of us is naïve enough to make the convenience of his own imagination a standard by which to judge the excellence of God's works. Yet however sophisticated we may be, we shall encounter difficulties inherent in the subject of our present discussion, which are likely to push us in the direction of some such absurdity, even against our wills. We sit down and we try to think about the creative intention which has made the universe what it is. We see that nothing worthwhile can exist, nothing which (to our human understandings) could seem to justify any creation at all, without a high degree of stable organization, whether it is the organization of stellar systems already mentioned or the atomic structure of physical substances, not to speak of the great elaboration of cellular arrangement which is necessary for plant or animal life. It is natural, then, that we should identify the will of the Creator with the development or preservation of system or structure, as unreservedly as we identify the intention of a human engineer with the construction or the upkeep of his machines. Any breakdown, friction, or interference in a system organized, must seem a setback for its designer, even where that designer is divine. Only that (we piously remind ourselves) God's resources both of power and of inventiveness are infinite, and he has all the time in the world. No setback for him can constitute a defeat.

Omnipotence must prevail; but we have still to ask, why is there anything for him to prevail against? If a human craftsman encounters similar difficulties, it may be due to the limitations of the medium in which he is obliged to work. But is there any medium in which God is obliged to work? Surely he must choose his own material, with sovereign freedom. If so, however, how does he come to choose a stuff which appears to be so recalcitrant? What engineer in his right mind, who had the choice of materials, would pick a soft and faulty metal, or pride himself on making an impossibly bad amalgam into something that would somehow work, though not for long, and not very well? What modeler would choose a clay apt to crumble under his fingers and to crack in the process of drying, for the vain pleasure of half succeeding with one work in a thousand, almost by miracle? The choice would be pure folly; and since God is all-wise, we shall not willingly admit that he ever chose so. Is he not more like the craftsman we would unreservedly praise—the craftsman who does wonders with poor material, when he has no option? May we not suppose that God's material was not chosen, but assigned to him by some prior necessity?

But what necessity could bind the action of God? What but a necessity arising out of his own character, a dictate of kindness, or of compassion? The Good Samaritan could not pass a wounded traveller without assisting him, and God could not see a pathetic muddle without bettering it. And whence did the muddle come? From the hands of inferior beings, spirits whom God created good, but who, by their own sin or folly, and the abuse of their free will, tried their skill at a creation of their own, and made a sad mess of it, a chaos of material forces quite out of control. Divine mercy then intervened, and began introducing a higher order, patiently redeeming by infinite contrivance the confusion which erring archangels had made.

A pretty tale, and we can say so without vanity, for it is none of ours; it is the ground plan of the great Gnostic Heresy, a theme on which endless variations were played in the second century by third-rate minds. In a certain sense, the Gnostics knew their trade. They let themselves go in novelistic elaboration, and edifying pathos; they interested the heart in a theory which, baldly stated, makes little appeal to the head; they charmed the imagination with labyrinths of mythic detail, and distracted the judgment from seeing the feebleness of the general design. For the weakness of the construction is painfully evident, if we are once allowed to attend to it.

The first point to strike us will be this: the theory abandons the broad and sane conviction that only God creates. That finite spirits, the creatures of God, have a limited power to manipulate God's creation, and often for the worse, is a fact we experience in our own case; and the orthodox Fathers, who refuted the Gnostics, assigned an ample part to the folly of fallen men, and the malice of revolted angels, in perverting the good world God had made. But God must make it, before his creatures could spoil it; whereas, in the Gnostic theory, they must make it before he could better it. Now it would be a satisfaction, certainly, to cast some light on the presence of evils in God's creation, but hardly at the price of confusing our perception that God created it. We can acquiesce, if we must, in our inability to fathom the reason of God's works; we shall not so readily part with our assurance that, however unfathomable, they are the works of God.

But the infringement of God's sole creatorship is not the last or the worst of Gnostic paradoxes. The doctrine supposes that the product of angelic error calls forth the compassion of God. He feels towards that unhappy chaos as, according to our revealed faith, we believe that he feels towards us; he would rather make it worthy of existence, than suffer it to lose it. The cases are not parallel, however. In our orthodox belief, man was made in God's image by God himself; and so it is credible that what frailty has spoilt, Mercy should prize. But before the God of the Gnostic fable sets to work on bettering the stuff created by erring spirits, what has it about it, capable of evoking his pity? Why should not he prefer quickly to let it drop out of existence, and create, if he desires to create, in a clear field and under happier auspices?

The Gnostic theory contains an internal contradiction. What it wants, surely, to say is that God finds himself confronted with a pre-existent material, so faulty in the grain that it impairs the perfection of his designs. What it is driven to say is that this material contains elements of such value that God himself cannot wish to let them perish. It must then go to the limits of mythical fantasy in explaining how, before God's saving intervention, jewels of heavenly worth came to be embedded in a rubbish spawned by inferior spirits. Even then, God's interest in the world must be confined to the heavenly pearls which so mysteriously had slipped into pre-cosmic dirt. His providential manipulation of material things will have the limited aim of delivering from them the nobler stuff imprisoned in them. He will not glorify the material order for its own sake, or on its own level. The pattern of the snowflake will not be the handiwork of God, but the offspring (we must suppose) of angelic folly. No wonder the Fathers of the Church accused the heretics of blasphemy and ingratitude.

The Gnostic Heresy is an old tale, and my readers may feel some impatience with me for dragging it into a modern argument. All the ancient theologians, you may tell me, thought they could explain much that is inexplicable, and hazarded speculations which laid them open to philosophic critiques. It is as easy to knock spots off orthodox Scholastics as off Gnostic heresiarchs; and neither sort of man is here to answer us. A contemporary mind which looked in the Gnostic or dualist direction might sympathize with something more like the following profession of faith.

"The supreme blasphemy is to attribute failure or negligence to God. But the flaws and breaks in his creative work are visible. I must therefore suppose that divine skill is doing the best possible with a pre-existent intractable matter. And if you complain that I deny God the sole glory of creating, by supposing the matter to be just there, I shall reply that there is no glory in the existence of brute stuff, and that what we mean by creation is nothing but God's artistry in working it up. If you challenge me to explain how the unworked matter came to be there at all, I shall answer that I do not know; and I shall give the same answer to your other favorite riddle, why, even it it was there, God used it, instead of letting it drop and working on something better. I should add that we go quite beyond our range, in starting such questions as these. Our minds are incapable of ultimate problems. We believe in God, not as the solution to a philosophic puzzle, but as a shaping and saving power encountered by us. We cannot see him, except at work; we cannot see him at work, without a matter to work upon. The matter he does work on appears in some degree intractable. We leave it at that."

There is much that could be said in criticism of this *credo*. We could challenge its despairing estimate of our mental capacities, or its oversimplified account of our evidence for God's being. But such issues are foreign to our present purpose, and we will concentrate on a single point. The great difficulty of any attempt to distinguish between a matter on which God works, and the work he does upon it, is to draw a plausible line between the two. Every theory of this sort must lean heavily on the simple analogies we mentioned a few pages back, comparing the divine Creator to an engineer at work with steel, or a modeler in clay. But, as we shall proceed to show, these analogies let us down at a vital place.

It is easy to draw a line between the structure of the mechanism, and the steel out of which it is constructed; or the clay which is modeled, and the modeling it receives. For clay or steel is mere material to the modeler or the engineer. The man is concerned with nothing about it, except its adaptability to the purposes of his craft. This adaptability is, as a matter of fact, grounded in the physical structure or the chemical composition of the steel or of the clay. But the engineer as such, or the modeler as such, is not concerned with the mixture of the clay, or the production of the steel. Either might, in a given case, act a double part, preparing his materials as well as employing them. There is nothing out of the way in the idea of a modeler's mixing his own clay; and an engineer might perhaps interest himself in the process which gave him a special steel required by his designs. But that is as far as he will conceivably go. He will take a hand in the blending of the iron and carbon, and whatever else goes to the make-up of steel. He will have no hand in the formation of iron molecules, though they too are composed of a prior material, just as steel is composed of them, and machinery of steel. Iron molecules are, in the eyes of human industry, a raw material cast up ready-made by the great process of the world. We do not need to make molecules, though we sometimes find it useful to interfere with them, manipulating the minute atomic structure of which they in turn are composed. Atoms themselves are not the bottom of nature; they are composed of electrons; and whether even these are primaries, is no question for a man so ignorant of physics as I am.

The engineer takes up a ready-made material, at whatever level he takes it up; whether he takes steel to make machinery, or whether he takes iron and carbon to make steel. The craftsman may receive his materials either from wild nature, or from human industry. If he receives them from industry, he receives what industry has worked up from nature, either directly or at some remove; we always draw on natural materials in the end, and so, for every human skill or craft, there is a pre-existent raw material. But can there be such a pre-existent material for the creative skill of God?

The answer will obviously be "Yes," if we are content to

speak from a strictly limited point of view. Even if the modeler mixes his own clay, yet as a modeler, and in the work of modeling, he employs a ready-prepared stuff. So God, considered as the maker of man, or of any creature above the lowest, can be said to work with materials already prepared, even though all the preparation has been done by him, at every level from the bottom upwards; even though he wove the electronic pattern, and the molecular, and any other there may be, whether precedent, intervening, or superimposed.

If, on the other hand, we take a comprehensive view of God's creative work, we cannot sensibly think of him as using a material absolutely pre-existent before any shaping or structuring on his part. The reason why we cannot, is not that we have embraced the dogma of God's universal causality, and so condemned ourselves to derive from God's own creative act the being of any matter he might use. However true the dogma may be, we have set it aside for the purposes of the present argument; for we are considering the hypothesis that all we know of God is the designing and shaping power by which he develops and perfects the world of nature. God works from the bottom upwards, but we, in this inquiry of ours, are going backwards and downwards, undoing the structure of nature level by level, and looking for what was there before he structurated any of it. What was there, then? It seems that, in dealing with this question, we are faced with an inescapable and ruinous dilemma. Either the pre-existent matter already had a structure of its own, however elementary, or it had none. And whichever alternative we embrace, awkward consequences follow. We will take them in turn.

The alternative most likely to attract us at first sight is that the original matter was without structure, pattern, or rhythm of any kind. For it is precisely the development of these forms of organization which (according to our hypothesis) constitutes the creative work of God. And it seems only logical to go the whole way, acknowledge God as what an older philosophy called the Universal Principle of Form, and assign all patterning to him, right back to the beginning and bottom of the world. What pre-existed was patternless stuff, on which the most elementary of all patterns was imposed by God's first creative decree.

The difficulty of this alternative is simply that the idea of a patternless or structureless material is without meaning, and indeed unthinkable. Our whole notion of a material to be worked upon is manifestly derived from human craftsmanship. Steel is material for bridge-building, or clay for modeling. And in virtue of what? In virtue of the structural characteristics either substance already possesses, and in virtue of nothing else. Because of its grain, or formation, the steel will take the strain, and the clay the impress. If neither clay nor steel had any minute uniform structure, neither would be material for any process rather than for any other. But for difference of material structure, we might make knives of butter, and ropes of sand. If the supposed pre-cosmic matter is structureless, no meaning can be attached to the statement that it serves as a material for God's creative act.

Is any defense possible in face of this refutation? Perhaps an appeal to God's omnipotence will save the hypothesis. Of course (it may be rejoined) God's raw material does not offer to his creative act the sort of support which our materials offer to our constructions. We can only construct on the basis of structure already present in the stuff we use. But God can and does impart to the raw material of the world all the structure that it ever comes to possess. After all, the hypothesis of a pre-existent matter was not put forward, because it was felt that God needed an independently existing stuff to help out his creative power. It was put forward by way of doing justice to the paradox that a creative power which is apparently limitless should be found wrestling with some sort of basic intractability in its objects.

Such is the defense; but it lays itself open to a crushing counterattack. If a structureless material can offer no support to God's creative work, still less can it offer any opposition to it. A stuff unsuitably structured could stand in the way of omnipotence itself, supposing that omnipotence were resolved to respect the structure it already had. But a structureless stuff (if such a stuff is thinkable) could not on any supposition hamper a power capable of imparting to it any structure he might wish. There is nothing more to be said, and we may as well pass on to the consideration of the alternative.

In accepting the supposition (we will now say) that all structure, even the lowest, is from God, we succumbed to the persuasions of verbal logic and deserted our bluff empirical principles. It looked verbally neat to write, "Let God be the Universal Principle of Form in things." But the tidiness of human formulae is not to be made the measure of realities unproved by experience. The God we encounter is the author of a marvelous and vital elaboration in natural being, effective on many levels, and open to our actual knowledge. If there is (as it seems there must be) an elementary pattern or structure in the lowest level of material existence, it may be nothing very wonderful, nor need we attribute it to God. It is just the way the lowest matter happens to be; but God, taking hold of it, develops it in accordance with its own way of being, by the application of his infinite skill, building level after level of purposeful structure on the elementary structure of original brute fact.

Here is a defense which sounds well enough, and makes a specious appeal to our empiricist prejudices. But the theory it proposes falls down on the true empirical test—we cannot work with it. We can say it over, like an incantation, in the study; we must forget it in the laboratory. Consider the predicament of the devout scientist, according to this doctrine. It is, we take it, conceivable that he should penetrate to the ultimate material level; and for the purposes of argument, we will suppose that level to be the electronic. So long, then, as he is observing the arrangement and interplay of atoms, he may, and should view them with that religious awe which God's handiwork demands of us. But as soon as he turns his attention to the electronic structure underlying, he must be careful to kick himself; must switch reverence off, and switch on indifference. For whereas the arrangement of the atoms was a miracle of divine adaptation, the swirl of electrons is that brutal and unaccommodating order which merely happens to be what it is, and opposes to creative purpose a hampering resistance.

It is not merely that such an emotional program as this would be psychologically difficult; it would be spiritually perverse. The very principle of religious empiricism on which the hypothesis claims to stand is that the divine Creator is to be recognised, where he makes himself to be acknowledged. It is monstrous, therefore, to fence off areas or levels of being on theoretical grounds, and to forbid men to acknowledge God there, even though he may seem to show himself. The most elementary level of physical organization, just because it stands on the confines of existence, and holds, as it were, the brink of not being, moves the religious mind to own the power that formed it. Wherever we try to draw the line between divine ordering above, and a mere structure of brute matter below, the distinction will be just as arbitrary, the doctrine equally incredible.

Either the supposed pre-existent matter was structured, or else it was structureless. The alternatives are exhaustive, and neither is tenable. We must conclude that it is useless to look for the cause of physical imperfections in the intractability of a basic matter, on which God, for any reason imaginable or unimaginable, is found to work.

CHAPTER IV

Physical Accident

"A very negative conclusion," we may say, looking back over the discussion we have just ended. What have we shown, but the uselessness of any attempt to blame a pre-existent intractable matter for the imperfections we find in God's creatures? And yet the argument has not been a blind alley of debate. For, in the course of it, we have become familiar with the nature of an evil, which we have vainly endeavored to explain.

What happens, in fact, when the material element inhibits the development of any form? Suppose that a plant is stunted by the structure of soil in which it takes root, and killed by the lower stratum into which it proceeds to strike as it grows—what is the nature of the trouble? The upper stratum yields materials deficient in certain components necessary to the plant; the lower contains a component actively hostile to its existence. In either case there is a misfit between the formal properties of the plant and the formal properties of many minute bodies composing the soil.

In an example like this, we may indeed diagnose the evil as bad matter; since the plant takes the soil as a matter for incorporation into its own system, and finds it unsuitable. But suppose another case; suppose the soil as favorable as you like, and attribute the poor plant's sufferings to greedy, choking weeds. Then the evil is not bad matter, but bad neighbors. Even so, more generally considered, the trouble is the same, a misfit between the properties of different systems placed in mutual relation: say, the ground elder and the strawberries. We may take a third case: the sorrows of the plant are due to animal pests. Here the matter-form relation is reversed. It is not that the sufferer ingests destructive matter; she is herself ingested as matter by other systems, and destroyed in the process. The misfit works differently here, but it is still a misfit. The plant-system cannot be fitted into the animal-system without undergoing disintegration. Were it not for the absurdity of the phrase, we might (still speaking from the plant's point of view) describe the evil besetting her as that of bad form.

The purpose of these examples is simply to illustrate a common formula. Bad form, bad matter, and bad neighbors are all cases of a misfit between the properties of different systems placed in mutual relation. To reduce it to a phrase, let us speak of the mutual interference of systems as being the grand cause of physical evil.

There, then, is our cosmic diagnosis. If it is right, it can scarcely be original; it cannot have escaped the eye of Omniscience. But if this is the general cause of physical ills, and if God knows it, why does not he remove it? Put like that, the issue sounds simple. Poor, limping world, why does not your kind Creator pull the thorn out of your paw? But what sort of a thorn is this? And if it were pulled out, how much of the

paw would remain? How much, indeed, of the creation? What
would a physical universe be like, from which all mutual
interference of systems was eliminated?

It would be no physical universe at all. It would not be
like an animal relieved of pain by the extraction of a thorn.
It would be like an animal rendered incapable of pain by
the removal of its nervous system; that is to say, of its animality.
So the physical universe could be delivered from the mutual
interference of its constituent systems, only by being deprived
of its physicality.

In thinking of the world as a something which might be
cured of its general evil, we are tempted to treat it as though
it were a single system, from which external interferences
might be banished, or internal incoherences eliminated; a
beast with a thorn in its paw or a fault in its digestion; a car
with nails through the tires or a misfit in the cylinders; even
a molecule of some substance, broken down by external pressure or collapsing by some internal disintegration. But the world
is not a system, it is an interaction of systems innumerable.

"Interaction" may be an awkward noun to describe the
physical universe, but it has the merit of being a neutral one.
It would sound better if we called it a society of systems; but
the term would suggest a mutual regard and peaceful co-
existence scarcely to be found. If we called it a battleground
for the systems it contains, we should suggest a general
hostility almost as false. We should not do justice to that
degree of mutual adaptation, apart from which the several
systems would neither have developed their existence, nor
maintained it.

Nevertheless, in the many and various interactions of the
world, there are innumerable misfits, vast damage to systems,

huge destruction and waste. Why is it so, if God is wise and almighty? The question remains, and we will attack it forthwith. We will use two approaches in turn, value and possibility. First we will ask whether a more smoothly fitting world would be better; and second, whether it could exist.

First, then, do we even wish to see the world tamed to a universal harmony? Naturally, we should like it to provide a safer and less galling habitat for us men; but that is not the question. The present stage of our argument is not concerned with our special interests. Let us keep mankind out of the picture; let us contemplate the natural order as in itself splendid or mean, monotonous or various, vital or inert, boring or intriguing to the mental eye, whether of men or of angels.

Is it not plain, then, that the elimination of conflict between systems, if it could be achieved, would be achieved at a price? If the universe is to be, as it were, not a jungle of forces but a magically self-arranged garden; if the several systems are to occupy just so much free space each as they need, without crowding their neighbors; if none is ever to incorporate any part of another in itself, except in such fashion that it preserves or even enhances the self-being of that other; then what sort of a world shall we have? And do we welcome the prospect? Gone will be that enormous vitality of force, which makes every system or concentration of energy to radiate over the whole field of space, every living kind to propagate without restraint, and, in a word, every physical creature to absolutize itself, so far as in it lies, and to be the whole world, if it can. It cannot, admittedly; and why? Because of interference from a million rivals, all equally reckless in their own vitality. Eliminate the mutual interferences, and gone, equally, will be the drama of an existence continually at stake, of a being which has to be achieved and held, of the unexpected and the improvised.

Could we bring ourselves to wish these characteristics of the world away, supposing that we had the choice? Perhaps we might, if there were no other way of making the world safe or stable enough, to allow the emergence of any systems except the most rudimentary. But it is not so; in spite of the degree of chaos which actually prevails, there are intricacies of order in the minute, and sublimities of structure in the great, sufficient for our highest admiration, and beyond the reach of our minds. It seems mere greediness to wish for more; and having so much, can we wish that what we have should be rendered secure by being tamed, or unaggressive by being devitalized?

Even supposing that we should like to see physical nature thus transformed, it may still be that the transformation is impossible; otherwise put, that no such physical world could exist. The question of possibility was, indeed, the second point we proposed to consider; and it is surely the more important. Strictly speaking, it underlies the first point, the issue of valuation. We cannot sensibly discuss the value of an impossibility, nor continue to wish for what is seen to be absurd.

To proceed, then, to the question of what is possible, and what is not, in the way of physical nature. Could the world be physical, and yet be free from those often disastrous mutual interferences which ravage it? Evidently the first thing to get clear is what we mean by physicality. Only then can we pretend to judge whether it admits of separation from that accidentality and chaos which we are tempted to deplore.

Philosophers, when called upon to define the physical, are inclined to proceed cautiously and skeptically. Something, they say, makes itself known to us through the impressions we receive in our senses; and in forming an idea of this "something," we use certain mental pictures or diagrams. We do not know, in any absolute sense, what the physical thing is; we must be content to discover how it can most usefully be diagrammatized in our formulae.

Such an approach as this will be very proper in certain sorts of arguments; it is useless in theology. The theological question is not, how it is convenient for us to think; the question is, what God has made; not, what sorts of impressions physical realities make in us; but what sort of an existence they have or exercise; what sort of creatures in themselves they are, irrespective of whether we observe them.

Ancient theology spoke of God as the Father of all his creatures, not only of those among them that deserve to be called persons. And though we now restrict the range of divine fatherhood more narrowly, we need not forget the truth for which the wider usage stood. All creating is a sort of fathering. Where it is not the production of persons by the supreme person, it is nevertheless the production of individuals by the supreme individual. God's personal creatures share his spirituality and answer his speech. His physical creatures express his actuality, and mirror his vital force. They are action-systems, for to act is to be; they are what they do, or what they are apt to do. Their action is their own; for they cannot be themselves, except by acting of themselves. Physical things are physical agents. When God creates physical creatures, he lets loose physical forces; and until he dis-creates them again, they will do what they will do.

Every level of God's creation is run by the creatures composing it; but only the intelligent know (even in part) what they are running. The atomic world is run by the atomic energies.

And it is a manifest absurdity to suppose that they can consider the whole, or even consider one another. They cannot consider anything; the principle of their action is simply that it should go on discharging itself.

The first and most elementary energies of the world, by their mutual action upon one another, constitute a diversified field of force which is both the space and matter of the universe. But for them, the higher systems with which alone we are directly acquainted would have nowhere to be, and nothing of which to consist. Whether there could have been a world sharing any of the characteristics we call physical, which was built on different foundations from these, is a question we are powerless to ask. It is true that our predecessors, both scientists and philosophers, conceived the elements of the world otherwise; supposed, for example, a system of passive atoms like minute billiard balls, scattered over a pre-existent space. But we, looking back on their world from our better knowledge, see it to have been not only false in fact but untenable in theory. So far as we can know, or even speculate, to consist of rudimentary interactive energies is to be a physical world, and to be a physical world is to consist of these.

The elementary energies are such rudiments of being, that we can scarcely attach value to them, or, if one is swallowed by another, think it a matter for tears; any more than we shall weep to see a little eddy in a running stream annexed by a neighboring eddy, or both of them lost in the main current of water. But creative skill has introduced higher forms of action, richer systems of being to organize the elements of the world. And these too, being real creatures of God, act of themselves, and from the principle of their own being; which is, to build and perfect and maintain their own organization, seizing on the matter which suits them, and resisting interferences. It is impossible to see how strife between them is to be avoided, if they are to run their own world in this active fashion. It is an old story, how trial and error, and the elimination of the unfit, have produced tolerable compromises between warring forms, and achieved an often precarious balance. This is God's masterpiece. Could it be improved upon in principle? Could we have a world in which unintelligent creatures were the real springs of action, and in which, nevertheless, they freely moved without ever one trampling another?

When we lament the mutual destructiveness of physical things, of what do we complain? Is it that unintelligent creatures are not like virtuous men, or indeed, better? Good men consider one another and, in Kant's pedantic phrase, never treat their fellows as mere means to the furtherance of their own purposes, but always at the same time as ends-in-themselves. Yet the best of men cannot extend such benevolence to all the sorts of creatures with which they share the field of space. Our stomachs ruthlessly destroy what they consume, and if we spare animals, we shall still butcher vegetables. Only pure spirits could be wholly non-destructive. How, then, should unintelligent bodily creatures be so?

But it may be that the standard by which we condemn physical nature is not that of rational benevolence, so much as that of mechanical perfection. Human engineers can construct quite extensive and elaborate systems, in which the parts are so adapted, that both waste and accident are virtually eliminated (except now and then). Why, then, we ask, has not the Creator engineered the Universe? Ah, but consider how utterly unlike to any mechanism of ours the Universal *machina* would have to be. The purpose of a machine is not that it should give the happiest scope possible to individual existences composing it. The purpose of a machine is to deliver the goods. What goods would a cosmic machine deliver, and to whom? Might the Creator have thought to glorify himself by constructing a cosmic gramophone, streamlined for the production of symphonic Alleluias? But that is not how, it seems, he thought to glorify himself; and he is wise.

The machines we make presuppose the matter out of which they are made. The matter has first to exist, by the free play of the energies composing it. That the matter itself should be mechanical, and the whole world from top to bottom a machine, is a senseless suggestion. Machines are certainly possible; bigger and bigger, better and better, machines. Machines are possible, as a special sort of order, artificially imposed on a careful selection from the wild variety of natural elements. Machines are possible, because men are actual, and because some men have turned engineers. God created the men, and he has at least permitted the machines. If he desires machines, this is how he makes them—by introducing into the world machine-making creatures. That God should create machines directly, or that he should weave the existing matter of the world into a single super-machine, is an idea as childish as that he once literally molded Adam from clay, like a potter making a pot. God does not make artificial arrangements, he calls creatures into being; and they act according to their kind, or according to their skill. For example, they may make machines.

If it were true that physical nature had to be redeemed by being mechanized, one can only suppose that God would usher into the world an engineer-messiah, to mechanize it. And he, no doubt, would need collaborators. As well, then, think of a messianic race, as of a messianic man. Here is a dream, indeed, for the prophets of space-conquest. Let man embrace the heavenly calling; let him harness the galaxies, control the traffic of the stars, and buffer celestial collisions. But let him not complain that God might have done the work for him by direct interference, and the use of heaven knows what invisible tools.

We had better pause, perhaps, for a little breath, and see what we have said. "If God was pleased to create a physical universe, he was sure to set going an infinity of forces and a plurality of systems, mostly devoid of intelligence, and acting upon one another in accordance with the limited principle incorporated in each. Such a universe must inflict much accidental damage on the systems it contains; a damage which is the essential form of physical evil." Does it follow that physical evil was unavoidable? Only if it pleased God to create a physical universe. Did he need to create such a universe? No: he did not need to create anything. But suppose he wished to create something, was he obliged to create at the physical level? On the grounds of revealed faith, it is plausible to argue the negative. Christians have commonly believed that God has created angels, pure spirits and supposedly non-physical; and it is our universal faith that he will immortalize ourselves, in such a way that we shall cease to be physical in the ordinary sense. On either argument, non-physical creatures seem to be possible; so that, even if God wanted to have creatures, he would not have needed to make physical creatures.

If such reasoning is accepted, we have not solved the problem of physical evil, by showing that a physical world inescapably involves it. We have merely pushed the question a

stage further back. Instead of asking why God did not make
his physical world free from its characteristic ills, we ask why,
since such ills inevitably characterize it, he made a physical
world.

What are we to make of the question in its new shape? It is
open to us to reject it, as totally unreal, and undeserving of an
answer. If that is the line we mean to take, we may argue as
follows. The problem of evil in any form only arises if we are
inclined to believe in God, and in his goodness. For it is only
then that we are moved to ask why, being good, he allows
evils to multiply in his creation. Now we should not believe
in the goodness of God, unless we were ready to acknowledge
our existence as a blessed gift; and our existence is inseparable
from its context, the world in which it is physically rooted.
Believers must be glad to be, and to be in the world; they
cannot, therefore, ask why God has done so ill as to make a
world essentially of this kind. We could only wish the world
had been made otherwise, if we could wish to be creatures of
another sort. But we cannot; we want to be ourselves; better
men, no doubt, and happier, but still men. We love our physical
being: we do not want to be angels; and to be human is to be
active in the world we know. Because we take the physical
creation to be good, we are outraged by the presence of certain
distressing features in it; but once they are proved inseparable
from its general nature, there is no further question we can
rationally ask. To regret the universe is either morbidity or
affectation. The pressure of immediate sufferings may unhinge,
indeed, the balance of judgement. Our derangement may be
wholly pardonable, but it must not be allowed to pass for
sanity.

We have taken a short way with impugners of the creation;

and it is at least arguable that it is the only sound way. Certainly if we attempt the long way, we involve ourselves in great unrealities. We should be undertaking to vindicate God for making the world as he has made it, rather than otherwise. But this would involve the serious pretense to conceive the predicament of Almighty Wisdom, in choosing what sort of a world to make. And is not such a pretense fantastic? If it is even right to speak of creation as the choice of a world, it cannot be supposed that such a choice is anything like the choices with which we are familiar. I can choose a wallpaper for a room. I can flutter the leaves of the pattern book, gradually narrowing my choice among the colors or designs which are at all suitable to my purpose, until I fix on one of them. I can do this because the shopman supplies a pattern book, with some fifty papers in it. But there was, for God, no pattern book of fifty, or of fifty thousand, possible worlds. The world he would make would be the world he would invent; and his powers of invention are inexhaustible.

Men also invent; artists, for example; and the process of artistic invention probably casts as much light as anything human on God's devising of the world. But there is one aspect of God's creative activity on which it casts no light at all; and that is, his preferring one possible creation to another. If we ask why the poet, or the composer, applied his talent to the writing of some particular work, rather than any other he might have written, the short answer will be, either that his previous history led up to it, or that the situation he saw before him called for it. For God's creative act, neither explanation is available. No situation confronted him, before the world was; still less had he undergone a personal history, such as might have directed his invention into one channel, rather than another.

The lovers of music or of poetry may, indeed, protest that neither the history nor the predicament of the great artist will account for the form of his creations. There is an element of sheer inventiveness which is his supreme glory, and his most godlike power. True, maybe, but of no assistance to us. For while sheer inventiveness may be godlike, it is not an explanation; not a principle pointing to the production of one work, rather than another. It is simply the ability to make both excellent and new whatever is made.

Once a work of art is on the stocks, and in process of construction, we can see (though we might not foresee) reasons inclining genius to develop it, and fill it out, in a certain manner. But the reasons, such as they are, lie in the beginning made, the sketch projected, or the skeleton already set up. The intelligibility of the choices which develop a project leaves the choice which first fixed upon it as unintelligible as ever it was.

All human analogy fails us. We can cast no light on the choice God makes in creating the world he creates, because we cannot, even in imagination, set up the experiment—cannot put the alternatives for selection on the table, nor construct the selective mechanism. What we feel bound to say about divine decision merely serves to put it beyond the range of human conceiving. God's mind, we say, does not labor, like ours, through a multitude of suggestions; he goes straight to the goal of his choice. He does not start with shadowy might-have-beens, and fill one of them out with the substance of being. He simply decrees what is; the might-have-beens are

accompanying shadows of the actual, the other ways in which
God knows he could have created, and did not.

We may say such things; we cannot think them. The
creator's choice is an abyss, where human thought drowns.
As in a dream, we spread our hands to swim, and find what
seemed water to be a thin vapor. Our customary strokes obtain
no purchase; we might say we were sinking, if the medium in
which we are were gross enough to be felt, in being fallen
through; or if there were any bottom for us to strike.

We cannot describe our Creator's choice as the act of the
God that he is. We can only describe it as the act of a man,
with whom we are pleased to compare him. No doubt, if we
make such comparisons, we make them for the sake of a moral
which we hope to be divine, in spite of the human basis of
our analogy. But we cannot be sure that the hope is justified.
We are at the mercy of our own parable, and if we hit on
any truth, it is more by luck than by method. It might be well
if we could refrain from inventing such stories altogether.
If we could—but we cannot; the urge towards mythical day-
dreaming is too strong. Since we have the dreams, it will be
wiser to narrate them than to suppress them. If we reveal them,
we can at least submit them to examination, and escape the
compulsive sway they might otherwise exercise over our minds.
We, for our part, will make the confession of our folly, and
write out a fable or two about the creative choice. Here, then,
is the first of them.

The divine Goodness desires the existence of creatures that
shall be excellent. Not, however, that shall be of the highest
excellence; for the highest belongs to the divine nature alone.
God fulfills in himself all that is possible on that supreme
level. To realize the divinest good, he has not to create, but to

live. But there are lower levels of excellence possible; and it
is better they should be filled, than lie empty. A gardener may
have filled the best beds he has, where the aspect is fair, and
the soil deep. He may still wish to plant other grounds, where
much beauty, though not the highest, can be brought to
flourish. So God plants over the next best soil available to him;
he extends existence to archangels, pure spirits though finite;
each a limited mirror of his own perfection, each viewing him
from a distinct point of vantage; each answering the vision
with a unique obedience. These beds being planted, the divine
gardener takes pity on the next best, and after those, on the
next best again; and so down through many ranks and hierarchies of angels, as far as the humblest sort of pure spirits.
These having been created, a fresh choice has to be made. All
the possibility of spiritual nature has been realized—everything
you could call garden soil has been brought under cultivation.
Only dry walls and rocks remain. What can the gardener do
with stones? He can slip little plants into the crannies; and
he may reckon it the furthest stretch of his art, to have made
such barrenness bloom. So, beyond the spiritual there lies the
possibility of the material. The creator does not hold his hand.
It is better a physical universe, with its inevitable flaws,
should be, than not be; and from the stony soil of matter he
raises first living, and then reasonable creatures.

The moral of the parable expresses a venerable doctrine;
and it is fair to admit that it is independent of the more
superficial absurdities which the gardener-comparison contains. It is obviously misleading to suggest that the possible
levels of creatures are fixed before God creates creatures to fill
them, in the way in which several possibilities of cultivation
are fixed for the gardener, by the qualities of ground in his

domain. The several levels of creatures are fixed by nothing but the act which creates them; for in creating them, God invented them; they were not to be thought of, before they were born. The absurdity of pressing the garden-analogy at this point is evident; but we need not press it. The moral is saved if we say that as the gardener chooses to plant inferior beds when the superior are full, so God decides to invent a further and lower level of creatures when each higher level is complete.

All stories about God, in so far as they are stories, show a common absurdity—they subject a timeless Wisdom to the form of time, and make befores and afters in Eternity. In the tale we have told, God was shown as thinking his way, stage by stage, through a descending creation. Yet the moral is not lost if we correct this childishness. Let God see, or invent, at a single glance the whole cascade of creatures, falling from the frontier of eternal light to the brink of blank darkness. The implied justification of our own material universe is unaffected. Whether proceeding step by step, or in a single sweep, God makes the material realm as a creation worth having in addition to many hierarchies of splendid spirits, and not as constituting in or by itself the best of possible worlds.

So far, the garden-parable has stood up to the criticisms it provokes; but there is a third wave of attack which is much more damaging. Whatever else in the garden-story may or may not be essential to the moral, one feature at least is so. The gardener's motive for planting worse ground is that he has filled the better; and God's motive for inventing on a lower level is that he has exhausted the possibilities of the higher. In the case of the gardener, the meaning of the suggestion is perfectly clear. His good ground is of limited extent, and it will not carry more than a certain number of rose trees. How familiar to the gardening amateur is the temptation to over-plant his beds! Far better throw that extra half-dozen roots away, or put them in waste ground, to take their chance. But why should it be supposed that the Creator's situation is anything like this? We may perhaps agree, for the sake of argument, that there is a best number of angels in any given angelic kind; by making more, God would not enrich his creation. But what should make us think that to find waste grounds of still unrealized possibility, he must move to a lower level? Why should there not be boundless spaces of open opportunity spreading in all directions at the same level? Surely infinite inventiveness could devise endless numbers of new kinds, all lying at the same altitude of being. Think of the animal kinds known to us. They do not fall into a simple series stretching from the least noble to the noblest. There are many equally noble, but in different ways. And what logical reason is there against an indefinably great number, all different, and all of equal nobility?

It is a baseless suggestion, then, that the Creator, wishing to go outside what he has done already, must go downwards. He might go sideways for ever, for anything we can tell. And so there is no reason why he should ever, in the invention of new creatures, reach the material level. And seeing it was precisely this that the garden-parable set out to explain, we must judge it to have failed entirely.

If we are to do any more storytelling, we had better try a different approach. If, by working through all levels from the archangelic downwards, we never arrive at our mother earth, we had better try the opposite proceeding, and show reason for beginning with the material universe. Our new question will be, "How far down did God have to go, to find a bottom on which he could build a creation?"

Put like that, the question sounds fantastically mythical; what it really means, we will hope to show as we go on. We shall begin by attacking the assumption that it is possible to begin with archangels. It may be right to think that God would gladly create beings as near as possible to his own perfection; but then they must be *beings*, with, as we say, a soul of their own, and an action which they exert of themselves. And we cannot be sure that the finite or created gods, who figure as archangels in old textbooks of theology, are far enough away from their Creator to be anything at all. What can their minds be, but mirrors of the divine thought; or their actions, but executions of the sovereign will? There is no real creaturely core to such a manner of being. Is not the idea of an archangel, thus conceived, the idea of a contradiction? Will God make archangels, any more than he will make square circles? The garden-story suggested that the archangelic nature might bloom beside the godhead, like a briar beside a rose. But perhaps it would perish in such proximity, like a rose in the shadow of a beech. We have told a story supposing the possibility of archangels. Let us tell one supposing their impossibility.

God's desire was to create beings able to know and to love him. Yet, in the nature of the case, there lay a dilemma. In proportion to their capacity for such love or knowledge, the created minds or wills would be dominated by the object of their knowledge or their love; they would lose the personal initiative which could alone give reality to their knowing or their loving. The divine glory would draw them into itself, as the candle draws the moth. You might say, "Why should not he shade the light? Could not God put a screen between himself and his creatures?" But of what would the screen consist? A screen, literally understood, is a physical barrier; and it screens a physical object from an organ of physical vision. God is a spirit; and the hypothesis we are examining is of purely spiritual creatures also. What sort of screen could God interpose between himself and them? And where would it stand? Nothing, on this hypothesis, would exist but himself and they; so it must either be in him, or in them. It could scarcely be in him. How could we dream of God's darkening his immortal being, or clouding the clarity of his thought, so as to baffle the search of his creatures? The screen, then, must be an obstacle caused in them by God. It cannot lie in the limited capacity of their organs; being spirits, they have none. Either, then, it lies in the limited capacity of their spiritual nature, or it lies in an artificial check imposed upon that nature; a baffling, a confusion of their intellectual faculty by the will of God. But it is incredible, surely, that God should create a noble faculty, and systematically frustrate its natural use. Rather than that, he would surely wish to make creatures whose own weakness and fallibility provided the necessary obstacle to an excessive enlightenment; silly spirits, so shadowy and slight that in spite of a purely spiritual nature, they would have little sense of God.

It seems a disappointing conclusion, and quite unworthy of the Creator's wisdom. That is not surprising, since in presuming to reason as we do, we are guided by our own wisdom, not by his. But, if we are to move at all in such a field of speculation, we can hope for no better guide; and, however absurdly, we will play out the play of argument by the light we have.

Since, then, the notion of a purely spiritual screen between creature and Creator has proved unhelpful, we may wonder whether we were not over-hasty in casting the idea of a physical screen aside. There cannot, admittedly, be a physical screen in the literal meaning of the term; for a screen must stand between physical senses and their physical objects; and even if God gives his creatures physical senses, he cannot make himself a physical thing. But suppose he creates a whole physical world, and places creaturely minds in it; suppose he so attaches them to it, that they are initially turned towards it, and find in it their natural concern. May he not then have strong animal minds, aspiring to know him in spite of their native physicality, instead of feeble spirits, whose obstacle lies in the mere poverty of their spirituality?

Might we perhaps say that the first requirement is to have a created world which is quite other than God? Then, by identification with such a world, godlike creatures may keep their distinctness from God, and not fall straight back into the lap of creating power. To express the idea, we borrow the pen of an ancient rabbi.

The Holy One (blessed be he!) when he sought to create the first Age, whereunto was he like? Like our father Noah, looking for a second Age, after the first had perished by water. He sent forth birds from him out of the Ark, and twice they returned. He said, "There is as yet no world in which to plant." He sent a third time, and the bird returned not. He said, "Dry ground appears," and presently, going forth from the Ark, he planted the stock of the vine. So likewise the Holy One, in the meditations of his creative thought, sent forth an archangel; and the archangel returned into the mind that sent him. After him, an angel in like manner; and the angel returned also. He said, "There is no ground in which they might root themselves." Then he sent forth a simple thing, without understanding, and so small that no eye but his (blessed be he!) could perceive it. And it returned not, not knowing the way; for in its simplicity it knew not anything. He sent forth another such, and the two clung together; and so another and another, multitudes without number; and they clung to the first. He said "A firm ground appears," and he set foot upon it. There caused he to grow up the garden of Eden. Moreover he took the dust of that ground, and molded our father Adam, shaping him in the image and similitude of God.

There is no need to point out the mythical character of a story like this. No one can seriously believe that the Creator, even in the realm of his own imagination, experiments with bad ideas before he hits upon good. All the parable really means is that what might have seemed good to us was left aside by God, because it was no good in fact. He simply began his creation at the greatest remove from his own perfection, and built it up from there towards himself, that being the best and most fertile method.

The story has the advantage not only of explaining why God should create at so low a level as the physical, but also of squaring with what we know about the world we live in. For, to all evidence, the world-process begins with the most elementary organization of energy, and builds gradually up, level by level. So we shall be likely to feel that the Ark-parable is altogether more enlightening than the garden-parable.

Is there anything to be said on the other side? We, who believe in angels and archangels on the authority of our religion, may be unable to accept a story which is based on the supposition that such beings are impossible. But the objection is not invincible; for the Ark-story need not absolutely deny angelic being. What it denies is that creation could begin with pure spirits, or that their existence could draw on the being of God alone. If they have one foot, as it were, planted on the material creation, the story has nothing to say against angels, any more than against mankind. For we, too, take hold of matter on the one hand, and God on the other. The hold of angels upon matter, or of matter upon angels, cannot be supposed the same as in our case. But may not their initial concern have been with the administration of the physical world, or with the guidance of its reasonable inhabitants? Angels, like men, may be freed at last from physical bondage. But they may have been so grounded in it first, as to obtain an individual existence; an existence which God afterwards liberates and glorifies, without destroying it. Belief in angels may be an article of faith; but we are surely permitted a great latitude of speculation regarding the nature of these mysterious beings.

A more serious point in favor of the garden-story may seem to lie in its estimate of the physical creation. The Ark-story attaches, indeed, the highest importance to it; but that importance is entirely negative. Matter is the screen before God's face, the other-than-his-being. Whereas the garden-story values it for what it is. Though a mere fringe on the great fabric of creation, it is also worth having, and that is why it is created; God lavishes upon it all the creative skill which its intrinsic limitations allow him to deploy in it.

The point may seem to us to be well made; but is it, after all, irreconcilable with the moral of the Ark-story? That story explains God's beginning his creation so far down; it no way forbids us to suppose that God values the lowest thing he makes, for all that is in it; or denies that he puts into it what none but infinite skill would be capable of. As the garden-story itself confesses, God would not have created the physical, but as part of a whole containing spiritual constituents. But in such a whole it has its own place, and its native honor.

We have told two stories, and rubbed them together. We could tell many more; but the more we told, the greater would be our disgust. There must be something radically false about a line of speculation which reduces the most august of mysteries to the triviality of a nursery tale. Consider any range of actual creatures in all their intensity of being, their intricacy of action, their mutuality of relation; and then think of the divine appointment on which their existence rests. Think of the will that can will such things, and you may experience the awe which authentic deity commands. But speculate on the reason why such-and-such existences have been appointed rather than others, and you fall into a silly, heathenish mythology, with no savor of godhead in it. Our first thoughts were best; we cannot swim in such waters. We may imagine that we have plunged, but we remain rooted to the bank, making empty gestures of swimming with our hands.

If we ask the question "O God, why did you make such a world as this?" we do not know the meaning of what we ask, because we cannot conceive the conditions, or rather, the unconditionedness, of the creative choice. All we can do is make up our minds whether or no we are grateful for the creative acts which have made us what we are, and put us where we are. There are many flaws in the physical realm, through the mutual interference of physical systems; but the interferences are such as a realm of this sort is bound to throw up. Any single adverse accident could have been prevented, if circumstances had been altered. But the alteration of the circumstances would have made other accidents. Accidentality is inseparable from the character of our universe.

CHAPTER V

Animal Pain

Animals, looked at from outside, are going systems, and parts of physical nature. Like other physical organizations, they both suffer damage, and inflict it. Kings, looking at cats, may observe what they do to mice, or what dogs do to them; very much as they may observe what weeds do to lilies, or lilies to weeds in the palace garden. But cats can also look at kings; the world is a cat's world, no less than a monarch's. And what sort of a world? When those alert, yet strangely impassive eyes sweep the presence, what impressions do they collect? Most of the universe is background to them, and the stage is narrow. Perhaps the curtains of the room are undrawn, and the night sky is open. Yet there is no depth of space; the stars are rubbing their faces against the windowpanes. Stars are lights, or fires; and such things are possible dangers. But these are outside the room, and very small. Nor are they in motion. The danger is, clearly, not imminent; they are hardly worth a notice, compared with the objects to be sought

or shunned within the compass of the room. The fire in the
grate is terrible, yet at five paces' distance there reigns a
luxurious warmth, conducive to repose. Better keep half an eye
open, nevertheless, for the spaniel between the royal feet; and
the royal hand, if otherwise unoccupied, may be good for a
saucer of milk.

The cat's world is a world of banes and blessings; blessings
to be embraced, and banes to be shunned. Pharoah's daughter
(so the Wise have informed us) brought King Solomon a
cat with her dowry. It happened once that the creature had a
bad day, and complained in piteous mewings of a world
in which the banes so far outnumbered the blessings. It was an
ill deed, she said, so to have created it. Her royal master
smiled; for it was given to him that he should know the voices
of beasts, and the song of birds. "Foolish creature," he said,
"how large a portion of this universe do you suppose cats' banes
or cats' blessings of any kind make up? Not the ten-thousandth
part of a ten-thousandth part."

Here the cat, who had never been able to count above five,
closed her eyes, and lost the thread of the discourse. But
the royal philosopher prolonged his admonition. "And what,"
asked he, "are cats' banes, or cats' blessings? They are not
sorts of things, that God has made so. There is, indeed, the
herb catbane, a natural kind like fleabane or henbane; but
that is another matter. What you esteem your banes and blessings are made to be such simply by relation to your appetites
or needs.

"To complain that the banes of existence outnumber the
blessings is like complaining that the inedible outweighs the
edible. Absolutely considered, the fact is past a doubt: most
of the universe cannot be eaten. But a man (or, indeed, a cat)

of sense does not attempt to eat everything he sees. He knows in what directions to look for his food, and reserves the epithet "inedible" for what, promising to be edible, proves otherwise. A creature who complains that the inedible predominates, accuses itself; it has not learnt to cater for its natural taste. It is the same with banes and blessings more in general. Folly moves in a world of misfortunes; common sense discounts pitfalls which experience has made it second nature to shun. Evils are only evils if we are uncertain of avoiding them. A tolerably prudent conduct will bring down the threats of our environment to a balance with the promises it offers, anyhow so long as we keep on our feet. And since cats always fall upon theirs, you will have difficulty in persuading me that this world is no place for your species. Your grudge against Providence is not just. Like your master, you are pampered. I have, it must be confessed, a taste too discerning in wine, and you in cream. Let us try again, however."

The monarch said no more; and those who were trained to interpret his wishes stepped forward with what he required. There was a cup for the king, and a saucer for the favorite. Solomon drank health to the cat, and the cat lapped satisfaction to herself. The cream was good. At the first taste she altered her philosophy.

Solomon was, perhaps, somewhat facile in his consolations. Some animals are genuinely unfortunate; the universe is not egalitarian. There are starving, persecuted strays as well as palace cats. Nevertheless, to complain that, in animal life as a whole, environmental evils predominate over environmental goods scarcely makes sense. The first function of consciousness in animals is to find the path of life, a path which needs to be found, a track of peace and plenty winding narrow and precarious among harms and scarcities. If animal skill, or animal instinct, does not bring evil down to a practical balance with good, the species perishes and the sorrows end.

The balance of goods and evils is a practical balance; the animal is not overborne by an excess of ills. There is no balance struck by anything but the creature's own existence. It would be absurd for an observer to aim at mathematical objectivity by counting blessings against banes. Even if he were able to decide what he should put in either list, and what omit, he still could not settle the issue by adding up the items. They would be of unequal weight; and to allow for this fact, he would have to give a figure for the specific gravity of each; say *plus* two for a good dinner, *minus* five for a thorn in the foot. And who could begin to take such figures seriously?

It may be said that if environmental goods and evils balance, nature is still not justified. For it is a sorry thing if animal life is no more blessed with goods than cursed with evils. And it would be a sorry thing, were it so; but it is not so, nor does it follow from the environmental balance that it should be so. Animal existence is beset by goods and evils, things needing to be shunned and things asking to be embraced. But animal action is the shunning of the one, and the embracing of the other; and while the animal survives, it is successful rather than the reverse. Success reduces threatened harms to forgotten fears, and raises promised advantages to the status of real satisfactions.

Living is its own justification, and its own good. An animal's attention is focussed on environmental values, for it is with environment that the creature has to cope. But animal good is intrinsic to animal being. The value of the creature's sentient life alone determines the values of those things which promise to help, or threaten to hurt it.

Such considerations as these, however reasonable, are unlikely to satisfy the compassionate heart. Assuming that the animal creation must be beset with threatening harms, we may admit the vindication of Providence, which lies in the actual triumph of life over danger. But why should we make the initial assumption? Why must the play of animal life be a dodging of death? It is in this hideous fact that the cruelty of nature appears.

Well, and what are we to say? First, that cruelty is a term misapplied. Nature is no malicious empress, presiding in an amphitheatre where creatures are hounded to their destruction. Nature is the general name for natural forces. Just as "man" has real existence in Tom, Dick, and Harry, so "nature" is actual in dog-nature, oak-nature, cell-nature, molecule-nature, and whatever other natures there may be. And what characterizes the natures of things (if we must moralize them) is not malicious cruelty, but innocent self-love. Their bent is towards the fulfillment of the pattern in which each finds its being. They are not capable of mutual consideration; in the pursuit of their own success, they trample their neighbors. How could it be otherwise?

The reader will perceive that we have fallen into the lines of an old argument. The exposure of animals to disastrous accident is a function of their physicality. It is superfluous to repeat for living creatures in particular what we have explained with reference to physical systems in general. For animals, whatever else they may be, are physical systems, and suffer as such the reign of accident.

"They suffer it, indeed," our friends may reply, "and what

is more, they perish by it. How can we accept the defense that they manage, on the whole, to thrive under it, rather than otherwise? You have said that while the animal survives it is successful rather than the reverse, in shunning evils and embracing goods. But this is no better than a platitude. While the animal survives, it is unquestionably successful in surviving; and you may claim, in addition, that survival normally carries certain satisfactions, such as opportunities of mating and palatable food to eat. But this is only so while the animal survives, and no animal survives for long. Destruction has the last word."

"Of course it does," we shall reply. "Your platitude is just as flat as ours, and platitudes seldom add real weight to arguments. Everlastingness is no more in the contract of animal, than of vegetable, existence; so why complain of timely death? Immortal dogs are no more to be looked for than immortal daisies. Adopted by us, animals obtain a sort of personality in human affection, and a man will grieve at the death of a dog. But that is a human, not a canine sorrow; and our present concern is with the ills of animal life, as they exist for the animals themselves. And though death, as you say, has the last word, the hand of death falls for the most part with merciful swiftness on the animal creation. How do swans perish? A friend of ours found a swan, otherwise intact, lying dead in his yard. She had flown over the city at sunrise, and her heart had failed. What proportion of her life had she spent in fighting her death? Many beasts have more violent ends. Yet do not they run with hope, until they are taken, and fight to win, until they are killed? Since animal fear is essentially the fear of death, when they are finally gripped by it, the terror may appear absolute; and this is not a pretty sight in human eyes. Yet the animal does not know it will die; it cannot tell itself, "The end is come. What overtook this and that one of my kind last month or last year is overtaking me today."

Or do we make our defense too easy, by taking the case of timely death? If we view the animal creation in all its breadth, immature deaths hugely predominate. The prodigality of life scatters embryo animals as it scatters vegetable seeds, to strike root where they can; and it is the few that reach maturity. Yet for the most part, their perishing is in an instant. How many of them ever were aware of good or evil? If, however, they have the joy of life, they have it; they do not know it will be short. Most tadpoles are food for fishes; but they have a lively time, until it suddenly ends.

We place the justification of animal life in a good intrinsic to life itself. We do not mean bare existence; life has a color, and if the color is wretched, the life is not on that level self-justifying. And it seems that nothing colors life more immediately than pain and pleasure. Pain is misery while it lasts; and even though there are happier hours to come, the infliction may seem gratuitous. Animals suffer an appalling amount of pain, on any showing; and it is often said that the agonies undergone by brute beasts are the most difficult of all facts to reconcile with a divine providence.

The statement expresses emotional reaction, rather than rational conviction. Reasons are, nevertheless, offered in support of it. First, the sufferings of brutes (it is urged) do not allow of the special justifications pleaded for the sufferings of men. Men are guilty of human suffering in a thousand ways. They neglect one another, or prey upon one another; they pamper themselves; they build up a vicious culture in which

the human animal could not be expected to thrive. Even where
we have not caused our pains by our misdeeds, we may be
held to have earned them by our sins. How few of us can
say, "I have done nothing to deserve it!" None of these justifications, whether they are sound or hollow, can be supposed
to apply to the case of unreasoning beasts. We cannot exonerate
their Creator by saddling them with moral responsibility.

A second type of argument indicts the uselessness of animal
suffering, by contrast with ours. Our ills can be turned into
good by heroic endurance. It is a commonplace that suffering
teaches moral wisdom; and some religious confessions make it
a dogma that personal pain can be offered as a sacrifice, to
the advantage of our neighbor. Whereas the sufferings of
beasts must be deemed perfectly useless, irredeemable by any
spiritual act or moral attitude.

A third argument is that irrationality aggravates pain. To
judge from our own experience, nothing but the power of
reason can render physical sufferings endurable. We can support the pain of dentistry by telling ourself that there is no
malice in the infliction; the man is only cruel to be kind.
Suffering the after-effects at home, we remember that, however
wanton the clumsiness of the operator, the agony he has
planted in our heads will die away in two or three hours.
Whereas an animal sufferer is all in his pain; he cannot look
beyond it. It is a horrid business to operate on a struggling
brute, whose fear you cannot allay, still less secure his co-
operation.

Last, the dumbness of animals is often alleged as an aggra-
vation of their lot; though this is rather a special consideration,
and hardly applies beyond the limits of domestication. Our
dogs are less likely, indeed, to get speedy relief than our chil-

dren, not being able to tell us their symptoms, or ask us for a remedy they crave.

It is possible to counter these arguments on their own ground with a good deal of force. While it is true that irrationality excludes rational mitigations, it equally excludes imaginative aggravations, and all too reasonable forecasts of pain or death. Animal suffering may lack the justification of moral guilt; but then less justification is required, where pain falls on a less sensitive, less godlike creature.

Yet the answering of the arguments point by point is really unprofitable. It distracts us from what is both fundamental and common to them all. For they reduce to the single observation that animal pain is sheer pain; and they ask us to agree that sheer pain is an unmitigated evil, incapable of justification. But is it? The issue we have to consider lies in the simple question, whether animals would be better off, if they had no pains at all.

Stated thus baldly, the question sounds outrageous. Of course an animal in pain is in worse case than an animal without it. Here is a poor, limping beast with a poisoned paw; there is another running free in the forest. We do not have to ask which is the luckier. It is better not to be injured or diseased. But would it be better, being diseased or injured, not to feel it?

By the time the medical faculty has assured itself of the diagnosis, and begun the treatment, pain has played its part and anesthetics are in season. They will spare us a needless agony and, by cushioning us against nervous shock, may even save our lives. But there is no medicine in the jungle, and animal pain must be set on a simpler background. Suppose that a sharp body is piercing an animal in the direction of its heart; is it better that it should feel its condition to be tolerable, or intolerable? Suppose it is weakened by injury or by disease; is it better it should aggravate the trouble by free exertion, or be deterred by pain? Suppose that sickness threatens its life. Is it good that it should run itself to death, or that it should curl up and conserve its dwindling vitality, because it feels too miserably ill to do anything else? Or suppose it liable to perish for lack of nourishment. May not a gnawing pain in the stomach play a useful part, whether by overcoming distaste for unusual food, or by inspiring an unusual effort to obtain it?

We might multiply questions to which the answer is equally obvious. To cut the matter short, we may boldly say that pain, and the remedial action which normally springs from it, are as vital as any functions of animal consciousness. Without them no living species above the most elementary would have the faintest chance of survival. Pleasure is a serviceable lure, fastening attention on the continued pursuit of a wholesome gratification. Yet we can conceive a creature capable of survival, which knew no positive pleasure, only the escape from pain. We cannot view as viable a creature knowing no pain but the lack of pleasure. It would perish in a thousand deaths.

Pain, then, is a natural institution which stands in no need of special justification. Pain, being the grip of a harm the creature has failed to shun, enforces the heed that was lacking, or evokes the effort that was unexerted. Even when the claws are not in us, the fear of pain, and the memory of encounters which sampled the ills we dread, will quicken the shunning of danger. Scalded cats and burnt children respect the hearth.

Pain is only wholesome when it is allowed its instinctive consequences. If we tie up an unanesthetized dog, and operate on it, we see a disagreeable sight. The natural effect of a cutting pain is to make the sufferer avoid the knife; avoid it, or else repel it. To cause the pain, while frustrating the resistance, is to inflict an agony beyond all reason. And since we, in our wisdom, have decided to operate, we blame Providence for a sensation both frightful in itself, and worse than useless in its effect.

Once we have seen what we are saying there will be few of us who will accuse Providence for not suspending the order of nature, to keep time with surgery. It is for surgery to do the suspending. Anesthetics must inhibit the sensation of pain, which the lancet would uselessly excite. But there are many useless and excessive pains in animals of which surgery is not guilty, and which anesthetics cannot reach; if we are going to complain about anything, we had better complain about these. The vital organs of brutes, no less than of man, can be rotted with disease, and the pain will tear them till they die. If the progress of the damage were unaccompanied by any disagreeable sensation, would they be any the worse? The agony serves no purpose but to prolong the agony; by discouraging free exertion, it saves them from working themselves to a speedy and merciful death. A compassionate man who happens to be armed, and finds a beast in such a state, will shoot it.

The utility of pain is unquestioned, but only on the whole. There is in nature a surplus of pain, as there is of fertility, or of appetite. This would be indeed surprising, if pain were a divine visitation, inflicted in each case for the special good it will do. But pain is a natural effect, and we have to consider the capacities of the natural machinery producing it. The machinery is subtle, and wonderfully adapted to its purpose; but how could the purpose be other than general? It is that damage should hurt, so that the hurting may provoke certain reactions, themselves useful in the main for preventing further damage. If there is damage, the machinery acts, whether or no avoidance is possible, or resistance destined to succeed.

If the wastage of unhelpful pain were to be avoided, the natural machinery would need to be gifted with foreknowledge, so as to switch itself off when its action is not destined to prove effective. But of all absurdities in this field, the greatest is to ask foresight of natural agencies. If the animal body is injured, it hurts, and the hurt animal fights. It does not know that the fight will be vain; still less do its pain-nerves know anything of the kind. Shall fibers feel a future which only the event will determine? The wisest of us, being witnesses to the occurrence, might be powerless to judge whether the animal was or was not certain to succumb. If it were a matter of calculating the further growth of a mischief already present, or the further effect of an injury already received, we might hazard a guess; though we find the learned physicians of our own bodies chary of prophecies. But suppose the issue turned on the action of external forces—whether, for example, a ravenous enemy would press his attack against a desperate defense. We could not have a moral certainty. Yet the pain the animal feels in being mauled, when it is destined to be devoured, is just as useless as the pain of a disease, under which it is destined to succumb. How can we suppose it possible that the alarm bell of pain should cease to ring, or the animal cease to resist its own dissolution, before the resistance is proved futile by being broken? Then, vitality failing, pain decreases; and the animal which has struggled fiercely dies quietly.

Perhaps a Christian reader, reflecting on what we have written, might pass some such judgment as this. "We do not

need a theologian to teach us the scientific attitude. We know
perfectly well that natural forces operate in accordance with
natural laws. But our Christian faith is that such forces are
tools in the hands of a Master; and what we expect of theology
is a little light on the way God uses natural agencies for the
special benefit of his creatures. So far, you have given us no
such light."

Here is a challenge which we must certainly take up. God
uses natural causes to bring about his purposes. All believers
will agree upon the formula; but they may not all mean the
same thing by it. The ambiguity lies in the word "use." A
dictator may use his countrymen's national sentiment to
secure his own aggrandizement; or, more laudably, use their
envy of a neighbor-state to stimulate their cultural development. Or again he may simply give employment to their inborn
skill, using it along the lines of its natural bent. In either of
the first two cases, the statesman twists a psychological force
to the promotion of ends it has no natural tendency to serve.
In the third case he sets an aptitude to work on its own
business, since the end he has in mind coincides with its
natural aim.

Now if we compare the statesman in his use of political
motives with God in his use of natural agencies, a difference
immediately strikes us. The political motives are there already;
the statesman must do the best he can with them. But the
natural agencies are God's own creations. If the statesman
were free to create the forces he was going to use, he would
not need to twist them. Suppose that his aim is to foster cultural
development. Had he the power to awaken unbounded enthusiasm for cultural life, he would scarcely prefer to implant
a dangerous envy against more civilized neighbors, for the

mere purpose of twisting it into a cultural dynamic. He uses the envy only because it is there, and because a sufficient cultural enthusiasm is not.

When God creates, he is not clearing up satanic messes. It is unreasonable to suppose that any of what he freely institutes is instituted for its oblique utility to other purposes; and it is impious on our part to justify his works on such principles. Every natural agent must find its justification in the action to which it naturally conduces. It is said that God overrules the work of certain agencies, in support to the work of others. But it must not be said that he created anything with one natural bias, merely to overrule it in some other direction. In human life, God may overrule the action of physical pain for moral ends. It is incredible he should have ordained it for that purpose, and not for the sake of its natural function in protecting our animal existence. Nor is this all. It is not simply that the purpose of pain must be found on the animal, rather than the moral level; it is that we must find it in the natural working of the nervous mechanism, under the direction of the principles it embodies. The mechanism must justify itself; we cannot require for its justification a perpetual miracle, making the incidence of animal pain the expression of a prescience and a wisdom which nerve-fibers cannot carry.

So far, we have said nothing very positive. God uses creaturely powers straight; he does not make them only to twist them. But how does he use them? We compared the Creator with a statesman who uses the inborn skill of his countrymen. He uses it straight, not obliquely. They have it in them to be craftsmen, or engineers, or inventors; and he finds employment for their powers. He does not simply set them to work, and let them do what they will do. He has a plan for the national production, and by taxes, subsidies, recruitment-schemes, propaganda, he draws the productive talents of the people into the service of his scheme. Their views are limited; each of them has or desires to acquire a craft, and to exercise it. Without necessarily initiating them into the mysteries of public economics, the statesman leads them so to carry on their work, that they further what they need not understand. In the same way we may try to conceive of creaturely powers each set in its limited aim or function, and yet drawn by divine skill into the service of purposes that are quite beyond its scope.

What would be the alternative theology open to us, if we rejected even so much divine overruling as this? Presumably it would be the absolute form of "mere deism," a textbook heresy which no one, perhaps, ever quite believed. The mere deist is supposed to deny any divine influence upon the working of nature, and to reduce theology to the bare hypothesis that behind all the natural causes we can observe, there is an unobservable First Cause for their being what they are. The world is like a collection of clockwork toys, once and for all invented, made and set going by God. Everything that has happened since that mythical first day, or will happen hereafter, is the simple effect of working forces put into the creatures —as it were, the interplay of the cogs and the uncoiling of the springs.

It is really inconceivable that anyone should even pretend to believe such a doctrine now. It was supposed to be a theology tailored to fit the sciences, and that is just what it will not do, as the sciences are now viewed. There never was a day when all the toys were wound up, and put on the floor—when all the species of creatures were let loose into the world. The world and its denizens have built up gradually, from primitive elements. If God is credited with having created, he is understood to have been at work throughout the process; "sustaining" and "creating" turn out to be all one. A "mere deist" was to hold that God once created, and now merely sustains his creatures without molding them. If we believe in creation at all, we believe that the molding goes on all the time.

In fact, we build one of our most persuasive arguments for belief in a creator, on this very ground. We call attention to the pitch of development which certain parts and members of the world have attained; and we point back to the elementary physical origins from which at the last remove we must suppose them to have sprung. Then we show the absurdity of pretending that the most rudimentary of physical patterns had it in them to produce what has finally evolved from them. And so we argue that the development must have been creatively guided.

So far, so good. But the next stage of the argument is more difficult. For, we say to ourselves, if the natural forces in position at the beginning were incapable of producing the end result, the whole development will be the effect of divine leading; it will be just as true that at any stage we like to take, the natural forces so far built up are incapable of achieving unaided the next phase of the evolution. But if so, we should be able to see just how far their natural tendency would have carried them; and how much further divine direction has in fact brought them. By establishing the gap between the two results, we should be able to define the creative *extra* which has been fed into the natural process.

It seems we should be able to do this. But can we? Apparently not. Inquiries along this line are all fruitless. The way in which natural forces are bent to creative purpose is so subtle, and so prefectly appropriate to the character of those forces themselves, that we cannot see what the *extra* is. The hand of God is perfectly hidden. We can never say what he does to the natural forces, to incline them as he does incline them.

It is true in general of the ways of God, that they first surprise us, but once appreciated, seem divinely right. To take the supreme Christian example, what more surprising than the saving Incarnation? Yet, once seen and believed, what more perfect, for the fulfillment of God's mercy towards us? Aristotle somewhere writes of a person whom he calls a servant-by-nature, a being with some capacity for seeing right reason, none for finding it. He would be scarcely human left to himself; by following the mind of a master, he reaches the human stature of which he is capable. Very likely there are such men, though probably fewer than Aristotle thought. But all men must be, in Aristotle's sense, the natural servants of God. We cannot find divine reason beforehand; we can sometimes, after the event, appreciate the inevitable rightness of what has been shown us.

The case before us is a case in point. We were inclined to think that the impress of the guiding hand on the forces of nature should be perceptible. We find that it is not; and having digested our disappointment, discover that we cannot wish it were. The perfection of the Creator's management of his creatures is shown by his ability to dispense with anything forced, anything adventitious, in his direction of them. Working in their own way, they do his amazing will. Our science never fathoms the subtleties of natural action, or exhausts the resources of natural explanation, so as to be in a position to say, "The overplus is Providence."

Our readers may feel that we are wandering from the point. We set out to look for the hand of Providence in the incidence of particular animal sufferings. Surely, we said, it must be unchristian to limit what Providence does for the sparrow to what its nerve-fibers have it in them to do. In pursuit of this inquiry, we have raised the general question of God's use, or direction, of natural forces; we have studied it in the wide panorama of the creative process, and the evolution of species. If we are to apply our conclusions to the question before us, we must descend again from the general to the particular. No one wishes to dispute that the working of animal pain has the rough effect of defending the species and promoting evolutionary development. The question is whether God does more for the individual's well-being, in the allotment of suffering, than the mere average working of the nerves will effect.

Our answer must be that in all things, and not only in the distribution of pain, God does more for the individual creature than would result from any calculations of natural law. In the study of nature, our science concentrates on rules or uniformities, and only concerns itself with particular examples in so far as they illustrate or test a rule. But general laws are not the real forces which compose the universe, any more than the Queen's Regulations are the Army and Navy. They are patterns of action exhibited by whole types of natural energies, and codified or diagrammatized by us. God does not make codes or diagrams, he makes creatures. The Queen (as it were) makes regulations, but God makes soldiers. He intends his creatures to act in the way of their kind, but he makes them individuals; it is as such that he knows them, for this is what they are.

When, therefore, God so imperceptibly and subtly directs

natural forces as we have argued that he must, if ever the world is to be made, he does not work with laws, or generalities, or averages; these are but fictions of the human understanding. He works with, and in, the real constituents of nature: particular processes, energies, or systems however minute, and to our way of thinking inconsiderable. As we rise to the higher levels of created being, this truth is still more evident, and certainly far easier to grasp. In bringing about the evolution of a biological species, God works through the multitude of individual creatures, by the sum of whose destinies the evolutionary change is realized.

The evolutionary theorist may be exclusively interested in the development of new kinds; God is not. How should we accuse divine wisdom of that worst human folly, which loses the end in the elaboration of the means; which, for example, views history as nothing but an infinite series of steps leading to a still unrealized utopian dream? Although in history one thing leads on to another, and everything (if you think so) to some final result, the whole tract of time is a field for the personal dramas of a million million souls. God is no less concerned for the individual, than for the future of the species. The life and activity of the single thrush or squirrel or grasshopper is a work of God.

Just now we were contemplating the miracle of the total evolutionary process, from its rudimentary beginnings to its highest visible development, as a manifestation of creative power. But to a sensitive mind, the miracle of the individual creature is just as striking and no less divine. Every sparrow is its own little self; it is no mere complex of general principles in combined action. God has made, and continues to make it. But here, as in the wider field, he works through natural forces and natural characteristics. Looking at the unique individuality and singular life story of any creature, we shall be unable to distinguish what comes by mere animal nature from the touch of divine direction imparted to it. Any fact or feature we can sufficiently isolate to ask why it is there will always appear to have a natural cause. The hand of God is perfectly hidden.

So God cares for the sparrow. Each bird is his particular creation, her vital effort a unique drama of his composition. But no natural regularities are violated, no natural averages falsified, no natural actions perceptibly supplemented by his creative work. Important among the factors molding the creature and shaping her life will be pains and pleasures. They are in the hands of God, but his hands are hidden in the workings of nature; and any *a priori* expectations we may set up, about what a loving Providence is bound to do in bending natural effects to kind purposes, will certainly be disappointed. The relation of natural force to divine will is an enormous theme, which we have not been able to evade, but have been still less able to explore. We have propounded dogmatically what we could not establish argumentatively; but we trust that, even without the supporting arguments, our conclusions will have commended themselves to the reason.

"To the reason, perhaps," our readers may reply, "but scarcely to the heart. The God you describe is an artist in creaturely existence; he is not the lover of his creatures. The care you attribute to him is a care over, not a caring for. A sculptor may take endless care over a portrait-bust; he cannot care for it, as he may care for his sitter, in providing for his comfort, or relieving his *ennui*. God does not make portraits of his creatures, he makes them, and their histories: things

over which care can be taken, but which equally can be cared
for. Yet your God does not care for his sparrows. When they
starve in a hard winter, either he does not grieve, or his grief
has no practical effect. And how do you reconcile either supposition with a faith which proclaims 'the Lord, the Lord God
Merciful, Compassionate' as the omnipotent master of the
world?"

The objection builds upon the distinction between two sorts
of care; and our answer must begin by reducing it. Does not
it break down entirely, as soon as we apply it to God? We can
show that this is so by taking each sort of care in turn, and
seeing how it coincides with the other sort. To begin, then, with
"care over." The sculptor can have no care for the portrait-bust,
and yet can have a motive to take care over it, because he wants
it, either for himself or for others. He wants it to be the expression of his aesthetic perception or artistic skill; for without such
an expression, he cannot exercise these noble activities. He
wants it to give others aesthetic vision or contemplative pleasure; for without such a medium he cannot communicate these
pure delights. He wants it to sell, and gain his bread; for with
nothing to put on the market, he cannot live.

Whereas God does not want his creatures for any ulterior
aim; he wants them to be, for their sakes, not his. Not, indeed,
only for the sake of each creature, taken severally; he wants
it also to serve or feed or delight or propagate others; but it
ministers to these aims indirectly, and by being itself first.
Since then God's care over the sparrow's coming to be, and over
its continuance in its being, is motived by his desire that it
should achieve and enjoy its existence, his care over it is
also a caring for it; as happens among us, when genuinely
disinterested elders educate the young. Their care over the

making men of them is at the same time a caring for them.

We have now to prove the equation the other way round, starting with "caring for." Let it be assumed that God cares for the sparrow. What form will his caring take? He will lovingly and heedfully benefit her. And how? By his creative action, by his continual sustenance and direction of her natural life. And this, as we have previously agreed, will be imperceptible to us, except in so far as it is manifest in the working of nature.

When Christ appealed to God's feeding of the ravens, or his clothing of the grass, he was not citing special providences. The tale of Elijah asserted that God had once made ravens carry miraculous loaves to feed the prophet. The Sermon on the Mount does not mean anything like the provision of miraculous loaves through prophetic hands, to feed the ravens. They are fed through the common ecology of nature. The things on which they feed flourish in their feeding grounds; and they have the wit, or the instinct, to feed on them.

To turn to our problem. The God of nature gives his animal creatures pains out of love for them, to save their lives; he makes the way of destruction distasteful to them, as a parent makes the path of danger distasteful to a child, by little punishments. Again, out of love for them, God moves his creatures to shun their pains and mend their harms, so far as their sense or capacity allows. And at last, when they must acknowledge defeat, as every perishable creature must, he relieves them of the power and will to struggle, of the pain on stimulus of which they can no longer usefully act, and of the being they can no longer hopefully defend.

One of the functions of pain, in species that are capable of it, is to awaken compassion. The suffering is felt to be a common evil; and as it moves the sufferer to get rid of the cause in himself, so it moves his kindred to get rid of it for him. For, by the force of sympathy, they feel it also. If there were no pain, no compassion would be excited, and the creature would lose a valuable source of succor in harm or danger.

We attribute pity or compassion to God. We cannot suppose that he suffers negative emotions. He does not need the compulsive pinch of sympathetic pain to make him do us good, his attitude is of a continual well-wishing expressed in a continual well-doing. But, speaking by human analogy, we use different terms to describe his love in several relations. In relation to demerit, we call it grace or favor; in relation to sin, forgiveness; in relation to suffering or misery, compassion. Were there no suffering in the creatures, there would be no sense in speaking of compassion in God.

God's compassion means, therefore, that he does not desert his creatures in those sufferings which his natural providence allots them, but is with them in providing the deliverance to which the pain excites them; which he does principally by sustaining and directing the working of their own natures; secondarily by the sympathy of their fellows in those species that are capable of it.

Men, though they are the greatest destroyers of animal life, are capable of sympathy with many species beside their own. When our compassion moves us to relieve animal suffering, we are being used by the compassion of God. Hurrying to the rescue, we feel that any being with sympathies equal or superior to ours must do the same, if he is within reach; and God is always within reach, being almighty. Why then is he not moved to prevent what we are moved to mitigate?

The question is not inamiable, but it is confused. God loves

his animal creatures by being God to them, that is, by natural
providence and creative power; not by being a brother creature
to them, as he does for mankind in the unique miracle of his
incarnation. He provides them with brother-saviors, or sometimes human saviors, through the working of compassion, and
not otherwise.

If we say that God, from the motive of compassion, should
have spared his creatures all suffering, we are surely talking
nonsense. It is only because God allots pain that there is
any object for his compassion, or any sense in speaking of it.

But the greatest fallacy in this whole field has still to be
mentioned. This is the suggestion that God's assigning of pain,
if admitted, provides a reason why we should harden our
hearts. On the contrary; every pain God assigns is a call to us
to remove the cause of it. God does not give pains that they
may be passively endured; he gives them to awaken our detes-
tation of their causes.

He provokes us to fight the causes; he cannot, within the
fabric of the existing world, prevent their arising. It must never
be forgotten that God is the God of hawks no less than of
sparrows, of microbes no less than of men. He saves his creatures by creating in them the power to meet the ever-changing
hostilities of their environment. And so, though individuals
perish and species die out, there is a world of life.

CHAPTER VI

Man Redeemed

So far we have proceeded in the main by the light of natural reason, and made few direct appeals to Christian revelation. We have been dealing with physical disasters or animal sufferings; and perhaps there is no specially revealed truth about either. Some Christians might say there is; but others, equally Christian, might deny it. It is otherwise with human ills. No Christian opinion can hesitate to hold that God's purpose in permitting them, and his kindness in curing them, are equally explained in the revelation he has given us. And it seems either absurd, or disingenuous in a Christian writer, to discuss the theology of man's misfortunes from any other starting point. We must first set out the saving gospel, and then the detailed implications for human sorrow.

Man, in being man, is both a body and a beast; he shares the good and evil of animal nature, and of the physical, too. From the incidence of the evils, he has no exemption; he has a greater ingenuity in palliating or preventing them; and this is all. But if he is a beast, he is a talking beast, and in his speech lies his reason. Through reason he shares, however faintly, that truth which is the mind of God, and becomes a copy or reflection of the divine likeness: in short, a person. Now the rational person offers an opening to God's mercy which humbler creatures do not. It is right that brutes should take their chance, and dogs have their day, according to the general nature of the world, and subject to God's manner of working in his whole creation. But the rational person God specially saves. Whatever our besetting evils, our frustrations, errors, sorrows, or defeats, he overcomes them. He attaches us to a good which comprises all goods, and in which all evils drown; a good no other than the vision of his countenance, and the society of his heart. The fullness of that blessing is promised for another life. But even in our present state, God is a sufficient support to virtue, and a sufficient consolation for distress. The spiritual man is saved from shipwreck here, and carried to the harbor of his hope.

Man is reckoned to be a fallen creature; his precarious condition has been lowered by his own perversity. But his needing to be saved is not the mere effect of his fall; it is the consequence of his animal nature. Man is not first an immortal soul; he is an animal on whom the capacity for everlasting life has been conferred. For he has been enabled to talk, and in acquiring speech has acquired the rudiments of reason. If you like, you can call him "nothing but a reasoning beast." Only you must acknowledge that no transforming magic was ever dreamt in fairy tale, to equal the gift of reason. The frog, released by fairy charms, becomes a prince; his stature, his physical lineaments are altered; his inexpressive face becomes the mirror of his heart, his speechless tongue the in-

strument of his mind. But then the story supposes that wicked
spells had overlaid the frog on the body of a king's son. The
frog had been a prince-in-duress, a rational person all the
time. There are, indeed, stories of another sort, where magic
turns mere animals into persons. But we are not then asked to
take their personalities seriously; it would be too much.
Cinderella's coachmen were mice transformed. They were
coachmen, but they were not men. They drove the pumpkin-
coach, and the whole equipage went convincingly. But it went
by the force of charms, not by the will or management of
persons who had once been mice. They neither loved nor
grudged their service; they laid no bets on the event of the
royal wedding. And no immortal souls perished when the
charm broke, and they were mice again.

The change which has transformed beast into man is of
another kind: an animal has become a person, and no prov-
ince or level of his conscious being has remained unaffected.
There is nothing distinctively human about the nerves conveying our pains, nor (we must suppose) about the feelings of
pain they convey. Yet I cannot have the mere experience of a
dog, or of a sheep, if I go barefoot, and tread a thorn into
my heel. The pain may be the same, the pain-experience
cannot. We never know a naked pain, we always take it as a
something—as a thorn, as a sharp intruder, as a danger, a
cruelty, an outrage; as burning, tearing, chafing, or disabling.
Our manner of taking it is human; it is colored through and
through with the habit of thought. We can take nothing as
we should if we were brutes, and had never learnt the trick
of speech.

The case of pain is not the strongest case we could take;
it is the weakest. If animal sensation is humanized by the

power of speech, how much more so are animal action, and animal emotion! We think of speech as our *Open sesame,* unlocking the cave of knowledge; and it is true that it offers to curiosity an infinite enlargement; not, however, to curiosity alone. The hoard which dazzles our eyes tempts our fingers, and what tempts our fingers, stirs our wonder. The world laid bare by reasonable discourse opens a field to all our powers. Not knowledge only, but love and delight find equally their objects; they gain that scope and liberty which make them worthy of their names.

Man, once endowed with speech, starts making an inventory of the universe. The speaker, having labelled everything else, labels himself, and becomes an item on his own list. He is now no more than a pebble on the beach, a part of the description he constructs; he falls under the net of an impartial rule, an equal justice binding on himself as much as on his neighbor. That justice is the child of speech, is evident; less evident, perhaps, that charity is; but no less true. If I talk, I can give a description of the world in which I am not the center. But equally, if I talk, I can give a description in which my neighbor is; can make him a focus, an eye, a heart, a man round whom the universe revolves; another self, an object of sympathy and concern. He is the center of things, just as much as I; but if so, neither he, nor I, nor any other man is *the* center. Speech makes a further advance, and spins a story in which our fellow creatures and we are equally the characters; and having reached that level, is found to be saying over, however haltingly, the speech of that creative Word, who commands the existence, and assigns the parts of us all.

Speech opens a path to knowledge, justice, and love, and even to the notion of God himself. Nothing that can be said will exaggerate the transformation of animal consciousness, which it has undergone through first acquiring and afterwards developing the ability to talk. Yet what is thus transformed is still an animal and, in being an animal is a physical thing. As a speaker and a reasoning person it is capable of an immortal destiny; as a thing and as an animal it is open to destruction and certain to die. Only the Creator who made us can rescue us, by making us over again in a stuff that will endure; and by so doing it that the thought and the person remain, though the substance is changed.

How God is to remake us is necessarily unimaginable to us. As the seed is to the plant, as the caterpillar to the butterfly, so, it has been said, is our present being to our future immortality. The parables cannot be bettered, but they are still wide of the mark. What God will do for us is God's secret; that he will do it is our faith. It is no part of our business in this book to prove that God raises the dead. We write for Christians, or for readers who wish to know what their being Christians would mean. We seek to unravel the mysteries of providence and evil which arise, once the basic belief of Christianity has been accepted.

How are we to balance the scale between spiritual salvation and physical vulnerability? Can we say simply that man suffers and perishes as an animal, while he is comforted and redeemed as a person? The distinction is neat, but is not it neater than the facts? We are reminded of the hackneyed line from Edward Gibbon; he sighed as a lover (he tells us) but obeyed as a son. He does not convince us; if the lover had sighed to good purpose, the son would not have obeyed, nor would the lady have been relinquished. Man is to suffer as a beast, and to be redeemed as a spirit, as though his animal sufferings left his spiritual being unimpaired; but they do not.

Sufferings nobly endured may be the gymnastic of the soul; but not every soul is in the position nobly to endure them. The soul, in this life, does nothing without a physical instrument. If part of the instrument is attacked or injured, the soul may withdraw into another part, and hold out against the damage, or repair it. The ordeal will be testing, but the response may be heroic. If, however, the whole instrument is maimed or twisted, especially the part vital to thought and feeling, then into what redoubt or citadel shall the struggling soul retire? With what brain, with what nerves shall she carry on the battle?

It may be that she is relieved of her post, and taken clean out of this bodily world. Or again it may be that she is not. It simply is not true that all men die as soon as their physical capacity for moral action is fatally undermined. Men die by inches, in mind as well as in body; and a gradual mental decay is not always a lapse, even, into a virtuous imbecility; it may be a corruption of character, and it may not (to any evidence) be specially the fault of the patient. It is a first principle of common sense in the nursing of illness that invalids cannot be relied upon for good behavior, and that the standard of conduct varies as much with the disease as with the person.

Common sense, indeed, is inclined to draw hard and fast lines between the condition for which we must make allowances and the condition in which our friends can be expected to be themselves. But in reality the hard-and-fast line divides between our attitudes, not between their states. We either treat them as responsible, or take responsibility for them; there seems to be no middle way for us. But there are any number of middles, or gradations for them, between psychophysical health and psychophysical incapacity. Men are not, in a spiritual regard, either fit or else bedridden. The world is more full of limping souls, who shuffle somehow about, than it is of birds with broken wings, or dogs going on three feet; and the fault may be just as physical in the one case as it is in the other.

We wanted to say that while men suffer and perish as animals, they are redeemed and saved as rational persons. But now it appears that the distinction cannot be drawn: spiritual redemption may be offered a person who lacks the bodily means to profit by it. And this is not the only case, though it is the most extreme, of physical obstacles apparently defeating personal salvation. By his identity with a physical body man is pinned down to a place in the physical system and made liable to all the cross-accidents which necessarily (as we have argued) abound in it. Such accidents may attack his health, and undermine the very stuff of personal life. But they may imperil his soul without doing this. One has only to think of a primitive community, whose livelihood is always on the brink of famine. It may be that, so long as they fight off starvation, the constant effort required, the anxious hunting and the sedulous digging, keep them in excellent health. Yet the unrelenting pressure of material need will surely narrow the affections, and cramp the spirit.

If such a predicament seems exceptional, let us take one which is unquestionably universal. Identical as I am with a mortal body, I am my father's child, and cannot choose my heredity. So far as I am concerned, I would not choose otherwise, if I could. As the Latin poet says,

While reason holds her throne,
I'll never grudge to be my father's son.

But others have not been so fortunate, nor reckoned themselves
to be so; and the harm accruing from bad parents seems often
irreparable. For, apart from any taint there may be in the
blood, there is the taint of thought. Our humanity itself is
a cultural heritage; the talking animal is talked into talk by
those who talk at him; and how if they talk crooked? His mind
is not at first his own, but the echo of his elders. The echo turns
into a voice, the painted portrait steps down from the frame,
and each of us becomes himself. Yet by the time we are
aware of our independence, we are what others have made
us. We can never unweave the web to the very bottom, and
weave it up again. And if the inculcated attitudes were warped,
or the suggested ideas corrupt, we shall never be rid of the
influence, and we may be incurably vitiated by it. Nor is it only
parental impresses of which we are the helpless victims. How
many persons, how many conditions have made us what we
are; and, in making us so, may have undone us.

If man is damned as a body, how shall he be saved as a
soul? It is a common though not always acknowledged observation that the gospel is preached to multitudes with whom its
acceptance is not a live option, or psychological possibility. It
is certainly more agreeable to fix one's eyes on the other side
of the medal, and consider the standing in grace of those who
have believed. Evidently they owe it to Providence, not to
themselves, if they are in the way of salvation. The Word
without and the Spirit within touched others as well as them.
The others resisted, they yielded; but the difference does not
lie simply in their good will, and the others' lack of it. It lies

just as much in a hundred circumstances outside the control of either parties. No one (to repeat the most obvious point) is praised or blamed for the choice of a father. Children are sometimes had by choice, parents never.

Believers are bound to see their standing in faith as the work of God; and they must acknowledge his hand in a physical providence, not only in a spiritual grace. It is not enough to recognize that Christ died and rose, that the Gospel was preached to us, that we were inspired to receive it. It must be added that God made us the men who were capable of receiving such a gospel, and of responding to such as inspiration. And how has he made us like this? By his whole way of working the infinite complexities of the bodily world.

Even this is not all. We shall scarcely be content to view the triumph of God's will as a mere *yes* or *no* matter, like the winning or losing of a game. We cannot think that he cares simply for the number of successes, and is indifferent to the individualities of those with whom he succeeds. That is not the moral Christ meant us to draw from the parable of the Great Supper—that the host is set on finding mouths to eat what his cook has prepared, and does not greatly care whose mouths they are. Disappointed by the friends he knows, he scours the highways and hedgerows for throats without faces. No; God is not content to make his saints capable of salvation; he has willed to make them the persons they are, each different, and each the inimitable handiwork of his creator. Peter was to be a Peter, and Paul a Paul; Bernard a Bernard, and Francis a Francis. But if God has made them so, it is not only by his supernatural and personal dealings with each of them. It is by his mastery of all the natural circumstances which have caused them to be the men, and indeed the animals, they are.

Here is a train of reflection most fit to stir up pious gratitude, or to awaken theological amazement. But, as we said, to contemplate such blessed mysteries is to look on the bright side of the medal; and we are concerned with the dark. If Providence has so ruled things as to breed a multitude of noble spirits, fed by happy influences, and enriched with shining virtues, then why has it been ruled that a multitude of others should be pinched and impoverished, agonized and cut short; and all this, it may seem, by no special fault of their own? Shall we blame once more the inevitable nature of a physical world? Shall we say that the soil out of which souls are raised is bound to be full of crudity and accident, yielding at the very best a patchy crop? But surely, if we do say this, we admit that God's saving work has failed—failed, anyhow, to correct the injustices of natural circumstance. Nature deprives millions of a full humanity; and Providence, by this account, lets millions more go without a saving knowledge of the Deity. And the painful conclusion is not bound up with any sectarian bigotry or limitation of saving truth to the area of Christendom. Even if we extend the scope of revelation, and add to our Savior Mohammed, Buddha, Zoroaster, Moses, and the Inner Light, the obstinate fact remains.

It is, of course, a possible move of argument, to cancel the difficulty at a stroke. We can simply call on a new world, to redress the balance of the old. Let it be granted that many men, or even most, go to their deaths without a saving knowledge of God, and with a nature more or less spoilt, a happiness clouded by adverse accident. What of it? They may all be new-minted after the image of God in a moment, in the twinkling of an eye, at the last trump. He who first made them may now make them all they would have been, if material circumstance had not proved intractable—all this, and infinitely more; grace upon grace, glory on glory may pour upon them from the hand of Bounty, as much as they will hold.

That is one sort of solution, but surely it is too easy; it sounds more like a cutting of the knot than an untying of it. The whole process of creation, so far as it affects mankind, is emptied of meaning, if God will make sinners into saints, and failures into successes, by an instantaneous act of will. If sanctity is not to be bred up in the world, but conferred by a wave of the wand on any flotsam the ocean of process happens to throw up, the painful efforts of the human spirit, and the love of saints in their co-operation with redeeming love, are left without importance. On such a hypothesis, God virtually makes the personalities he desires to have, on the day when he raises the dead; and we cannot conceive why their first making, through the whole vast process of the universe, was ever undertaken.

Will it help if we bring Satan in? If we say that God meant to make his saints grow naturally out of the world-soil, but that the devil (or some other interfering cause) came in and spoilt the crop? Such a supposition will not clear our hypothesis of its difficulties, anyhow if we are Christians. For our faith teaches us that God has not been content to let the devil have his way with us, so far as this life is concerned, and simply to cancel the effects of diabolic malice, when he raises us to another. No, God has come to defeat Satan in the field of this present age; he has redeemed many souls in their bodily existence; and it seems a lame thing to say, that the redeemed being still too few, he sweeps up the remainder by an act of omnipotence; rather as though as angler, after fishing all day with patient skill, and making a disproportionately poor catch, should open a sluice, drain off the water, and take up with his hands from the dry bottom whatever fish had eluded his hook.

The idea of a wholesale redemption on the last day may shock us, because it is inconsistent with articles of faith; or, more generally, because it suggests a procedure unworthy of God. But these are not the only grounds of objection. We may be just as much offended by the meaninglessness of the idea itself. Does the notion of so arbitrary and sudden a transfiguration of mankind even make sense? The immortalization of our animal humanity is hard enough to conceive, even if we die saints. We are to put off flesh and blood, we are to be remade in the stuff of glory, and still we are to remain ourselves. Where so much is changed, something must continue, or the thread of identity will snap. The disposition, the will, the person indeed, so far as personality can be distinguished from its physical embodiment, must surely persist. If the soul which history and circumstance twisted or stunted is virtually to disappear, while a full and straight personality is somehow fashioned from its elements, then in what sense is the new man continuous with the old? Has God saved his handiwork, in any worthwhile way?

A piece of worn embroidery may be saved by being remounted on a fresh piece of silk, in which case it remains the embroidery it was. But suppose it is unpicked, for the sake of the gold thread it contains, and the thread used to work a design on a new piece of stuff. In such a case, the old embroidery has simply perished, and something else has been made of the materials. Whatever we suppose about God, we cannot suppose him to need old materials out of which to make new spirits. If he transforms and immortalizes human beings, it is out of love or pity for them; and it would be a strange sort of love which destroyed its object in the process of bettering it. This is not what we know of God's revealed ways. So tender is his concern for our fragile identity that he studies to convert us to him by gentleness in this present life and lead us step by step to glory, as one who knows how much, in any case, glory must burn away from the body it transfigures.

We cannot accept the hypothesis of a sudden universal transformation after death; and so the paradox it was introduced to palliate remains on our hands as contradictory as ever. On the one hand we wish to say that God does not leave human personality to take its chance in the great whirlpool of the world; he specially saves it. On the other hand we are driven to admit that in spite of God's saving action, individuals must take their chance with the physical vortex. For multitudes are so stunted by circumstance, so blinded by inherited attitudes, or so cut off from spiritual light, that there is no presumption of their salvation through any saving action which God has made manifest. What we are trying to do, and have so far failed to do, is reconcile the preciousness of souls with the wastefulness, or prodigality, of nature. Some religious thinkers, such as, for example, the old Jewish author of the apocryphal *Fourth Esdras*, have been content to say that worrying over the preciousness of lost souls is a mere infirmity of the human imagination. The doctrine can be modernized as follows.

The divine Sower sows his seed broadcast; he does not grudge the wastage of it, so long as he obtains a sufficient crop.

He sows the field of space with elementary forces; like the seed, they have to take their chance. None of them, indeed, is simply lost, but only some of them combine in heavenly bodies. Yet, whatever the proportion of waste, God gets his crop of stars. He wants a soil for organic life, and here at least the wastage is enormous; the stellar universe is largely barren. Nevertheless here or there—we do not know in how many corners—revolves a fertile planet. Organic life is sown, and not the individual exemplars only, but whole kinds, both vegetable and animal, take their chance; a million species prove unsuccessful, and perish with the mammoth or the dodo.

These successive sowings are all in a manner preparatory, to provide a soil for the Word, the seed of reason; and in this view most of the organic species, however physically successful, are wasted; only one of them proves able to talk. And so we reach at length the last act. From within the talking species God recruits a company of immortal spirits. The word of the Gospel, the seed of eternal life is scattered, but like every other sort of seed, it takes its chance. What is best is rarest, and there are few so conditioned that they have ears to hear. Nevertheless, God is content, he gets his crop. It is as foolish to lament the wastage of souls, as to lament the wastage of stars. There is no injustice, no one is artificially debarred from salvation. The offer is open; all may accept it who can and who will. Some men cannot, it is true. But then, no horses can; and if we are not to lament the fate of the whole equine race, why lament the fate of half the human? No single soul is marked down for perdition. Just as we can labor for the health and cure of any man, so we can for his salvation. While there is life there is hope. And we shall have the assistance of God. The divine husbandman desires to gather all the good corn he can from his human field.

If it is asked why Providence must be content with so modest a proportion of success, Esdras can fall back upon conclusions already outlined in this book (See above, Chapter IV). The very idea of a creation, we suggested, implies that what God creates should be genuinely distinct from himself, and instinct with an action of its own. The elementary forces first created act each by the limited principle of its own being, and without regard for any wider purposes which God may entertain. It is only, therefore, through the most subtle and patient overruling of random accident, with an infinity of apparent wastage, that Providence draws the higher forms out of humbler patternings. The process is repeated (Esdras will say) at every stage of the upward development, and even at the highest; though the word of God is addressed to all, it takes hold upon the few. For God's will is to make heaven out of earthly materials, so that it may preserve a being genuinely distinct from his own. And this means that the recruits for heavenly life are appealed to, not forced; they continue to act of themselves, and after their natural kind. The appeal itself cannot strike home to all, conditioned as they are; and those who feel it may still refuse it.

If we are to refute Esdras' calm and satisfied despair, we must attack the last stage of his argument. We must resist his assimilation of the scattered word to those natural sowings which preceded it. Words are not sown, they do not strike root. What really happens? We are inclined to say that words are simply a medium; mind communicates with mind. And so it is, no doubt, when adults and equals exchange discourse. But that is not the case which the seed-analogy is employed to illustrate. When adults talk to infants, they evoke, or implant, the mentality which understands their speech. And something of the same sort happens when the saint speaks with effect to the spiritually unawakened. In such cases as these, mentality, or a higher level of it, is imparted, or at least actualized, in being addressed. This is what is meant when it is said that we learn to talk and think, or to talk and think at a new level. Though, on a given occasion, the lesson may fail, mentality can still be learnt at any level, so long as there is a teacher, and something teachable. When a seed is thrown away, a life-principle, a plant in embryo has perished. When a word is thrown away, nothing has been wasted but an opportunity, and someone's pains. So long as men exist, and God exists, there are the teachable and there is the teacher.

"Yes, no doubt; but there is small comfort in this reflection, if men, though ideally teachable, prove actually unresponsive to the divine teacher, and this by force of circumstances, rather than by any fault of their own."

Well, they are unresponsive in this life; but we are supposing throughout that God raises the dead.

"We are supposing it, certainly; but we have also argued that he raises them the same in personal being as they were before they died. Unless their whole set of mind is to be altered by their change of existence, why should they respond to the divine teacher any more in another life than in this?"

Surely the answer is obvious; because the lesson will be plainer. They will meet incarnate God in open glory.

"Yes, that is what a Christian will presumably say. But are we free to say it? For have not we insisted on a solution which will allow its due significance to God's attaching of men to his divine life, in the days of their mortal flesh? If confrontation with incarnate glory is to convert on the last day all people capable of good will, the mission of the Church in this world surely loses the crucial importance which our faith accords it."

Not in the least. The mission of the Church is concerned to build up that incarnate glory, which will shine with convincing splendor in the world to come.

"Please explain yourself. This is a dark doctrine indeed, and it sounds like a novelty." It is certainly no novelty, but the most venerable part of tradition. Whether it is dark or not is another matter; we will do our best to pull it forward into the light.

It was the primitive faith that the Son of Man should come on clouds, and every eye should see him; even the eye that clay had sealed, or flame reduced to ashes. And it was held that he would not be seen in solitary splendor, but accompanied by ten thousand holy ones, and king among the saints. What had been hidden—the life of Christ in mankind—would now be revealed; in an aureole of glory they would see the *Corpus Mysticum*, both Head and members. Our first Christian predecessors, persecuted and despised by the world, dwelt naturally upon the reversal of empire which that confrontation would represent. They saw the princes and the mighty wailing and deeply mourning for their error, when the Church, the mystical Christ whom they had pierced, was throned in the sky; when they were found to have been wounding the only power ultimately worth conciliating, or able at last to kill and make alive. Yet however just the picture of guilty terror, the mercy of God is not measured by the anticipations of human fear; they pray that the mountains may fall on them, and the hills cover them, but the everlasting Shepherd takes into his flock all hearts that have been tender to him in any of his disguises; who have fed the hungry, clothed the naked, or succored the miserable.

Though modern Christians may disown a literal belief in any such sign of fear or wonder due to appear on a calendar day, or to fill a visible sky, they will be ill-advised to let go the substance of an expectation which can alone make luminous to them the purposes of God. The Day of Judgment is not a confrontation with naked deity—and indeed, how should naked deity confront us? God is everywhere, or nowhere; his ubiquity is a general truth, and not limited to the conditions of mortal life. To see God, it is not enough to die; we must be made to look at the place where he has lodged himself, and at the created person with whom he has clothed himself: that is to say, at Jesus Christ; and where Christ is, there are the saints he has united inseparably with him, the members through whom his life is extended and expressed.

The substance and core of heaven already exists, built up by the patient Providence and the gentle Grace of God out of earthly materials, through the prodigal scattering of his word and Spirit. The traditional name for the chosen community was Israel. While the best inspired oracles of ancient Jewry held out a final hope to all mankind, at the same time they guarded the special vocation of the twelve tribes. Israel was built up into a people of God in this present time; the age to come, setting Israel on the throne of empire, would give all nations the opportunity of adhering to a society on which God's blessing was so visibly bestowed. Christianity did not (as is sometimes falsely supposed) abolish the distinction between Israel and the Gentiles; it drew it in a new place, by changing the method of recruitment for the Israel of God. It had been recruited by natural descent in one people; now it was to be recruited out of all peoples by Christ. The new Israel was to be no less separate than the old from the mass of mankind; it would continue to supply the core of heaven, and the touchstone of judgment. The Gospel closes no gates of mercy which the law left open. If the abundance of the Gentiles might be converted to Israel on the Last Day, so they may be also to the Church. To enter the mystical body in this life is not the only path of salvation; those who have not been able to see Christ in the world may acknowledge him at the last confrontation.

It has been a dogma that after death there is no room for repentance; that we settle our eternal future by the conduct of our present life. This dogma (let it be said, for the benefit of those who hold it) is not contravened by the hopes which we venture to embrace. To find our way into the Church is not the only way of finding salvation here below. We may so live as to make ourselves the men who will both recognize and love the Church, that is, the mystical Christ, when revealed to us in glory; who, recognizing and loving it, will be capable of assimilation to it, through the transforming company of its members—not to say, of its Head.

Our way of stating the traditional Christian hope is open to an obvious objection. The last judgment, it will be said, and the ultimate salvation of mankind lie in confrontation with the person of Christ himself. The saints, Christ's mystical members, need not be thought to play any essential part. What Christian can doubt the all-sufficiency and sole sufficiency of Christ, to act on the last day as savior and as judge? We must agree that no Christian can doubt Christ's sufficiency; but it is still allowable to ask how it takes effect. Christ, once revealed in humility, is now to be revealed in glory; and it is all too easy to acquiesce in the pictorial suggestions the word evokes. We see a person, larger than human, throned in an aureole of light. He speaks like the voice of many waters; the thunders of the firmament answer him. Surely this is nothing but metaphor. What else in fact is the visible glory of Christ, but the company of his redeemed?

In essence it must seem that the two-sided fact of last judgment and ultimate salvation lies in a confrontation with the Supreme Being. But, as we have already insisted, to meet God, it is not enough that we should die. God, out of his invisible omnipresence, must gather himself to meet us in a form we can recognize. And how he will do this, Christians are not left to conjecture; they know. God revealed himself in the human body of Jesus, and in that same person he will visit us again. But in what form, through the pages of gospel story, does the Godhead already stand revealed? If we have two lanterns, in one of which a light burns, while the other is unilluminated, we see the difference immediately. But as between Christ, in whom the Godhead shone, and John the Baptist, in whom it did not, there was no such visible difference. Christ was not a mystical saint so incandescent with the graces of contemplation that he must be acknowledged a person of Godhead; and it is indeed scarcely intelligible how any holy incandescence should evidence such a fact to the eyes of sinful men. Christ shone in his transfiguration, but it was a single episode, and it was not the basis of the gospel. The divine life which radiated through him took effect in words, deeds, and sufferings; a saving action developed in discourse, and in mutual dealing with friends or enemies; more especially with friends. The Christ of the Gospels can only be known through what he did, and in the doing of it. And how shall the Christ of Advent be known, but through what he has done, and the possession of it? If Christ's glory and godhead were at first manifest in his saving of men, and in the men he saved, how shall these things be manifest at last, but in the men he has saved, and in their being at one with him?

To put the point a little more philosophically. We speak of the incarnation of the Godhead, his taking of human flesh. Such a fashion of speech emphasizes the height of the miracle, and the depth of the condescension: God brings an animal nature into personal identity with himself. But the flesh is not the point of union; the divine action does not fuse with the throbbing of Jesus' pulses; it fuses with the movement of his mind. And mind in man is a cultural or social fact. It cannot arise in isolation, and it has its natural being in mutual discourse. God could not become incarnate in a human vacuum, and neither can he remain incarnate so. How justly, then, are Christians called the members of Christ! It is not only that they cannot find their perfection, except by subordination to such a head. It is just as much that he cannot live as a human person, without his person being extended and expressed in such members as these. What we are saying has nothing to do with the heresy, or rather, the blasphemy, which declares us men to be necessary for the completion of the life of God. No; God need never have created us, nor, having created us, need he have redeemed us, nor, perhaps, need he have redeemed us by becoming incarnate in us. But since he has been pleased to become incarnate, he needs the stuff and the embodiment which are involved in a true incarnation; that is, he needs the mystical Church, with which he will appear on the Last Day.

It is time that we recalled the problem which launched us upon this highly theological and traditional exposition; and that having recalled it, we should see what sort of a solution our orthodoxy affords for it. The problem was how we were to reconcile two principles. First, heaven must be genuinely made out of earth, without forcing the natures of the earthly constituents, a process which seems impossible except through much prodigality or wastage of materials, the materials in this case being human souls. Second, salvation must effectively embrace all rational persons who are willing to have it in the shape in which God offers it. What, then, is the reconciliation or solution we propose? It is this. The highly selective or (as we have called it) wasteful process really takes place within the field of human history. But what this process is designed to effect is not the general salvation of mankind. It is the completion of Christ's Incarnation. Christ is made whole in head and members; this is the Israel of God, the core and substance of heavenly being, a reality sufficient to act as the touchstone of judgment for all the souls of men, assimilating to itself and embodying in its own life those who are found able to respond—and none will be found unable but by their own fault.

The last thing, perhaps, that my readers would expect to find in a discussion on Providence and Evil, is a piece of dogmatic theology centered on the economy of salvation. Has not the author digressed? In his own view he certainly has not. The summit of the argument is the soul, or reasonable person, and the multiform evil threatening it. In the case of lowlier creatures, we are content that through an inevitable prodigality of nature the Creator's designs should take effect. In the case of mankind, our hearts are not contented so; and our faith comes to meet the disquiet of our hearts, with the assurance that God intervenes to save everlastingly as many as do not refuse. It is only in relation to God's general redeeming action that we can discuss the mystery of his ways with particular men; or how he saves their happiness through, in, and out of the miseries that beset them.

CHAPTER VII

Adam and Lucifer

How hard it is to please all parties! As we wrote the end of the last chapter, we became aware of critical eyes boring into our back, and turned to apologize for going so far with traditional theology, in a discussion like ours. But in making the apology, we felt the disturbance of other eyebeams, equally critical, and equally searching. How are we to hold up our heads to friends of ours, and learned theologians among them, who are amazed we should write six chapters on the problem of evil, and scarcely once mention the devil, or the fall of man? Their complaint is that we are not half traditional enough.

One can hear the scorn in a familiar voice, indicting our supericiality. "Mere sophistry," he says, "and special pleading. It carries no conviction. The plain fact is that the world we know, the world as it affects mankind, is all wrong, and not as divine goodness either made it, or could have made it. Do not justify the world. Accuse Satan, accuse those who have taken part with him. And praise the Son of God, who intervenes (would we but let him) to destroy the works of the devil. Half-belief and rationalistic optimism are condemned by their position to the absurd maneuver of arguing black into white. Full-blooded Christians stand on firmer ground. If we do not work from diabolic malice and original sin, we are throwing away our best defense, and betraying the revealed truth."

What are we to say to this? First of all, we must block the insidious appeal to prejudice which identifies extremism with loyalty. No one is a wholehearted friend of the workers, unless he is an out-and-out communist; no one a true Catholic, who is not an enthusiast for Papal autocracy. So no one is to be a genuine theologian, who dissents from St. Augustine or St. Thomas. It will not do; no one can be a true anything by upholding what he judges to be false.

Our next move is to distinguish between the two traditional doctrines which are being pressed upon us. The devil is one thing, original sin is another. If we deplore the state of affairs, and are unwilling either to shoulder the blame ourselves, or to saddle our Creator with it, we might shift it to our ancestors' back, or we might shift it to Satan's. Admittedly the traditional tale combines the two lines of evasion. Satan initiates the calamity by his rebellion against God. Our ancestors fall victims to his temptation, and so hand us down an inheritance of sin and guilt. As for us, we are perverted or enfeebled by original sin, and therefore lie open to Satan, who still goes up and down as a lion, seeking whom he may devour.

But there is no need to combine the two themes in this manner. If Satan could inexplicably revolt against his own happiness, and throw heaven away, so could Adam; the story can start with him; we have no need of Satan, to tempt him to it. And if Adam, in his virgin state of soul, could begin to sin, how much more can we continue in sin, vitiated by our inheritance of guilt? There is no need to bring Satan into the story. While on the other hand, if we make Satan the arch-villain of the piece, and credit him with the power of perverting Adam from his innocence, we must credit him equally with the power of perverting us from ours. We can be born innocent too; we need derive nothing by inheritance from our unhappy ancestor, in order that we should lie open to Satanic wiles.

The Adam-theme and the Satan-theme are essentially distinct, and we will take them separately. To begin, then, with Satan. Not that Satan stands for a single issue, either; the name covers at least two different questions, which we must in turn distinguish. First, does Satan offer a useful explanation for the origin of sin in general? Second, are there particular evils in the universe, better explained by the action of demonic malice, than by any other agency? We will take these two questions in order.

The first question is the more theoretical. It asks, how could sin have begun?—the suggestion being that it could more easily have begun with devils than with men. But why? The children's answer is, "Because we know that people aren't so bad: they always seem to be good at bottom. But devils are reckoned to be bad through and through." This merely shifts the question. How did devils get that way? For we are not to suppose that there were always forces of evil, set over against the forces of good. That is the dualistic heresy. We must on the contrary believe that God made all things, and made them well. If there are evil spirits, they are spirits created good, and gone to the bad. The common opinion is, or used to be, that they are fallen angels. Is it easier to suppose that angels should fall, than men? Manifestly not. Lucifer's fall, by which he became Satan, is not the most natural, but the most monstrous of imaginable sins. He has no fleshly nature, no wayward bodily desires to confuse his choice; and he has all possible clarity of spiritual light to direct him. That is why, while Adam can be forgiven, Satan cannot.

"Nevertheless," it may be contended, "Lucifer's sin is imaginable. That is why it remains a telling moral illustration. Man himself can sin in his most angelic part; those who seem to have left behind the infirmities of the flesh, and to be living in the Spirit at the very gates of heaven, can turn sanctity into pride, and go further from grace than sensualists. The corruption of the best is the worst. The sin of Lucifer is the typical sin, because the blackest."

Very well; but Lucifer's sin is only imaginable in so far as it is human. We can see the human will, of itself and on its own motion, committing the perversity of Lucifer; otherwise we could not imagine Lucifer's acting so. And even then we cannot imagine it, or certainly not as we can imagine the human case. We spoke just now of man sinning in his most angelic part. But man, in his most angelic part, and in his dealings with heaven, is still the same bodily creature. He is not a pure spirit, even on his spiritual side. We can conceive to ourselves the predicament of a mystical saint, tempted to pride, and we can see by what motions of the will it is possible, all too possible, for him to fall. The predicament is a human predicament, the fallible thoughts those of a bodily man. You can write a novel about it, and the page will live. You cannot do the same for Lucifer, in the pure altitudes of heaven. You will only make a story of him in so far as you humanize him.

"Of course," says our traditionalist. "What you say is so

obvious, it does not need saying. But it misses the point
completely. We know human nature; we don't know devil
nature, except by remote analogy. But that's just it. We know
human nature, and how golden it remains at bottom. We know
also the appalling perversities of human choice which (as you
say) are our only clues for understanding diabolic choice. We
men seem to make such choices of our own motion, or they
would not be choices. Yet, in view of what we know of the
human heart, we must suppose that they are the effect of a
hidden and malign influence, emanating from a spirit wholly
lost to goodness. After all, good men are often influenced by
worse men without realizing it; so why not men by fiends? And
if you go on to say that the malice of fiends is not so intelligible
to us as human malice, we of course agree. A malice absolutely
black cannot be understood by us. That is why we have to
house it in a creature who is, in the nature of the case, beyond
our proper comprehension. This is what scripture calls *the
mystery of iniquity*."

Well, if we meet mysteries, we ought not to talk them away.
But to suppose a mystery, or a half-mystery either, can scarcely
pass for the offering of an explanation. We may recall John
Locke's fable of the Indian. Asked why the earth remains
poised, he replied that it rested on the back of a giant elephant.
Asked on what the feet of the elephant stood, he replied, a giant
turtle. Asked the same question about the turtle, he replied
that he had not thought of that. But what the Indian meant,
we may suspect, is rather that he did not need to think of it.
A giant turtle, on whose back the feet of a cosmic elephant
might be supposed to rest, would be something quite out of
this world, about which you could think what you liked. It is
so delightfully remote, even more remote from us than the

elephant. As to the earth, the Indian was clear that it was made of soil and rocks, stuff that would fall unless it had something to rest upon. But about a cosmic turtle, who could say? Admittedly you had no picture of it but what common-or-garden turtles might suggest. Turtles, at least, would float in water—but a cosmic turtle—surely, to be a cosmic turtle, it would have to float in space.

Even as we have reinterpreted it, the Indian's reasoning is scarcely worth the trouble of pulling to pieces. We shall agree that, by mere weakness of mind, he is evading the conclusion, that the earth must be able to swim in space, as well as any cosmic turtle could. And it is surely the same with the origin of sin, perversity, or malice. To cast it back into the limbo of the unimaginable is not to explain it; it is merely to evade the effort of thought or the moral courage required for understanding it in the place where we can come to grips with it, that is to say, in ourselves.

Perhaps the argument we have used is too philosophical for some readers. So let us supplement it with something more religious. To refer again to those profound theologians, the children—they want to know why God doesn't kill the devil, and it is notoriously difficult to answer them. The grown-up person feels in general that the question is childish. It is not the sort of thing that God does anyhow. After all, he didn't kill Hitler or Judas or Caiaphas or Pontius Pilate. But it is not clear that the parallel offered by human villains is relevant. If God does not annihilate wicked creatures by a special intervention, we can give two reasons for this. First, they are parts of the natural world and, indeed, of the physical system; and the divine method is to draw divine purposes out of the world by a hidden overruling of its natural processes, not to force those purposes upon it by artificial violence. Second, the person who is a villain in our eyes is a soul in God's, a soul whom, perhaps, he will still save, and who in any case must be allowed to run his course and take his chance in his natural habitat.

Neither of these reasons will explain why Satan should be left at large. He is not supposed to be a soul of whom there is still hope. For if he is, then he is as mixed a creature as we are, his malice is no blacker or more settled than ours, and he adds nothing to the explanation of evil which human nature fails to supply. And even supposing that God respects his own handiwork, however perverted, and lets Satan live on, like the damned souls in hell, why should he be let loose on us? The damned souls are not. Our world is not his natural habitat, or at least he is no part of this physical system: it would be no breach that we can see in the order of nature, if he were banished to the furthest and emptiest part of space.

It is difficult to admit that Satan helps an inch towards explaining the origin of moral evil, or of spiritual perversity. Real mysteries, as we have just said, ought not to be talked away, or glibly rationalized; but the mystery of iniquity is not Satan, it is the sinful human will. Why do I ever refuse the better choice? Because the worse is attractive. "*That* is my duty; only *this* promises pleasure." Very well. But I know that the promise of pleasure is not so worth realizing as the duty is worth performing. How can I refuse what I see to be the greater good? And yet I can. However much sand your devil may cast in my eyes, he does not obstruct my seeing the greater goodness of the good I refuse. If he did, he would have missed what is taken to be his aim—he would have failed of leading me into mortal sin; if he really blinded me, I should be innocent of going against visible light. Or again, let him tamper

not with my vision of the alternatives, but with my act of decid-
ing between them. Let him influence, let him incline the
balance of choice all he can. If it remains a choice at all, I still
need not choose the devil's way; yet I do. The whole mystery of
iniquity lies in my perversity, a mystery which the supposition
of diabolic malice does nothing to clarify.

Perversity is both utterly inexplicable, and perfectly simple.
It is inexplicable, because it is perverse; how can you rationalize sheer unreason? It is the one irreducible surd in the
arithmetic of existence. Non-rational acts, like those of blind
passion, can be explained by natural causes, as can the actions
of beasts. Sensible decisions are explained from the reasonable
grounds which motive them. Innocent mistakes may be explained by a mixture of the two; there are the reasonable
grounds on which the mistaken man proceeds, and there is
the interfering natural cause, the fatigue or the prepossession,
leading him to misinterpret them. But nothing can explain
wicked perversity; nothing can explain why reason, supplied
with rational grounds, should willfully falsify her own procedure in relation to them.

Perversity of choice is willfully poor in the matter of reasons;
we cut ourselves off from the grounds of explanation by being
perverse. Perversity is simple with the simplicity of idiocy, or
of the mind which refuses to think. And yet it is different from
either; idiocy and the abdication of thought both leave the
field open for the operation of natural causes, the overflows
of passion or the automatisms of habit. Perverse choice is a
real cause, creating the effect, but a cause which cuts itself
off from reasonable grounds. It is both miserably simple and
hideously effective.

Being so poor and thin a thing, the perverse choice is not,

of course, really creative. All it does is to side with a rotten motive. When we say that it is inexplicable, we do not mean that it lacks motivation. The man who chooses to indulge his lust rather than to please his Creator, obeys the motive of lust; what is both motiveless and inexplicable is his choosing to obey it. There may be biases in the mind, additional to the simple attraction of lust; previous habits of sinful choice, the strong persuasion of another's will. Without motives, no one would be perverse; but the perversity of a choice which accedes to them, so long as any power of choice remains, is itself causeless and motiveless.

If we meditate a little on human perversity, we shall see that it can do all the devil can do in making an absolute beginning of evil; and this at every moment of time. The fable of Lucifer is certainly instructive, but it instructs us in the nature of human sin, not in its causes. At the last point, perversity is motiveless, it throws away the greater good to embrace the less; and the moral is made more evident if we make the last point the whole story; if we suppose a spirit enriched with all the joys of heaven, favored with the love and vision of God himself, unbiased by bodily desire, unblinded by ignorance of principle or of fact; if we suppose such a spirit, preferring the sterile satisfaction of pride and self-will to the inexhaustible wealth of a participation in the life of God; then we see without obstruction what perversity is—the perversity expressed in any and every sin.

Lucifer expresses our sin, he does not explain it. All that diabolic temptation can supply is motive, or bias; and here the demonic hypothesis is more than superfluous. We have motives and biases in plenty deriving from natural or historical causes. There is scarcely room for Satan to squeeze any more in.

Or do you disagree? Perhaps you think that there are motives or forces of evil in the world which cannot plausibly be traced to the action of natural agents, whether human, bestial, or inanimate. If you do, then you have a reason for supposing devils, which is independent from any attempt to account for the origins of human perversity. We said, in opening the subject, that demonology had two branches really distinct: the origin of sin in general; and the origin of particular evils in the universe, such that the action of a demonic malice would more plausibly explain them, than any other agency. We have now said all we wish to say about the first branch of the subject; and we turn to consider the second or more empirical line of enquiry.

The empirical demonologist is free to suppose that there is no essential difference between demonic and human wickedness. Let every sinner be the Lucifer of his own soul, and, conversely, let every devil be the Adam of his. The power, or shall we rather say, the liability to sin is inherent in a finite free will; inherent, therefore, just as much in angels as in men. Still, even supposing that there are angels, none of them need have sinned themselves into being demons. They need not; but, says the empirical demonologist, it appears that they have. For there are disturbances visible in the order of his world, which none but fallen spirits could have produced.

It must strike us immediately that the demonology of Scripture is mainly of this kind. Devils are credited with conveying monstrous suggestions to men's minds, such as they seem themselves incapable of entertaining; with giving effect to black magic, and all supposedly supernatural events not referable

to the Spirit of God; with producing the phenomena of aliena-
tion in the speech or action of the insane, and with causing
nervous disorder, sudden and inexplicable sickness, or even
sickness in general. The demonological theory about such evils
was no mere speculation, it provided recipes for dealing with
them. The essential point of diagnosis was not (let us say) to
isolate the bacillus, but to name the demon; for if you had
named him, you could exorcise him.

Since we have long abandoned the practical part of the
doctrine, it seems odd that we should trouble our heads over
the theoretical. Here or there in a nasty corner of the world,
in the witchcraft of primitives or the satanism of degenerates,
we come upon a spiritual stench which wakes ancestral terrors.
But surely we ought to keep our heads. What reason have
we to suppose that the resources of science—of abnormal psy-
chology, perhaps, or parapsychology—will prove ultimately inadequate to the phenomena we observe?

Speaking broadly, we should say that empirical demonology
was the child of scientific ignorance. It provided a language
in which matters beyond the reach of contemporary science
could be mythically described. It was better to attribute the
motives of madness to an infesting demon than to hold the
unfortunate sufferer responsible for them. The rationalism of
the day, by denying diabolic possession, might fall into a
cruel injustice. In reading demonological passages of Scripture, or other ancient books, we shall often be reading what
we recognize to be facts; but not facts about demons.

Scientific ignorance invited a belief in demons, but not
ignorance alone. We have also to reckon with the effects of
a false knowledge. It was not merely that the ancients were

at a loss to explain nature; it was partly that they explained it on wrong principles.

It was very generally thought in ancient times that the whole system of natural causes could be understood by a naïve analogy from human action. A man picks up a stick, and with the stick he dislodges a stone. The stone moves, but only because the stick pushes it, the stick moves, but only because the man wields it. And so we come back to the man. He acts of himself; but then he is alive, and conscious; he does what he does because he means to do it. It was assumed from this simple example that all things which act on others either pass motion on, or originate it. If they originate it, they are alive, and in some degree purposive or even intelligent.

It was also very generally thought that there tended to be a hierarchy in the order of causes. Men do not only handle inanimate things, they employ slaves or domestic animals, creatures supposedly inferior to themselves. And so, outside the sphere of human action, it was assumed that simpler agents would be under the direction of nobler and more intelligent beings. Surely the supreme cause of a star's movement (for example) would be nothing inferior to an angelic spirit.

It is obvious that a theory of this kind must incline to a cosmic optimism in glaring contradiction with facts. If the supreme natural causes are the most intelligent, and the less wise are subject to them, while mere bodies exert no independent force, being the passive instruments of soul, it is to be expected that the great system of the universe will move like a well-drilled army, and everything be for the best in the best of all possible worlds. Men looked into outer space and saw the squadrons of stars wheeling with such precision that their positions a year hence could be plotted by arithmetic. They looked nearer home and saw a system of which the general frame remained firm, while earthquake and tornado, plague, pestilence, and famine raged within it; where living creatures, instead of conducting themselves like the denizens of a royal park under the charge of angel-keepers, multiplied beyond reason, preyed on one another, attacked their natural superiors, and ravaged the habitable earth. Even under their own skins, men felt the pervasive disorder. Physical passion, which should be the dynamic of wisdom, had become the fuel of rebellion.

It seemed plain that something had gone wrong here under the moon. Either the superior spirits had changed from benevolent princes into wicked tyrants, or the inferior had thrown off their allegiance and forgotten their discipline. In simple fact, a theory which began by endowing natural forces with angelic virtues was driven to adulterate them with every human imperfection, so as to square their supposed conduct with undeniable phenomena.

What is the use of raking up these old-world stories? Because, however dead in theory, they are alive in our emotions. When the spiritual-minded or the tenderhearted nowadays complain that nature is too bad to be natural, and that the physical order is fallen, what makes them think so? Or by what standard of the ought-to-be do they condemn the things that are? My sympathy supports the lament, but my reason derides it. For I do not believe any of the propositions required to give it substance. I do not believe the purposiveness of natural agents, the hierarchy of causes, or the inertness of matter. I think that God's creation begins from below with a chaos of non-rational forces, each acting of itself with inexhaustible energy; and I view the degree of order and the complication of structure which Providence has drawn from these beginnings as a miracle of patient overruling. The marvel is, the chaos is not more.

It is a popular aphorism that the devil's cleverest maneuver was inducing us to disbelieve in him. The meaning of the remark is that we shall be ill-prepared to resist an undermining corruption which we are persuaded to ignore. And there is practical truth in this, if the alternative to a belief in Satan is an ill-founded confidence in our own rational processes. To deny Satan may be to suppose that we have nothing to fear from detached psychic forces in our own souls or in other men's; forces which may wear the guise of a subhuman malice and of an instinctive cunning; forces of which the minds housing them may be largely unaware. To ignore such forces is certainly dangerous, and it is better to call them "Satan" than to disbelieve in them. But suppose we do believe in them, and, not content with believing, wish to understand them. We shall follow their action better if we view it as a sort of cunning, than if we view it as a sort of natural force. Only, in the interpretation of the cunning, we shall be largely led astray if we call it Satanic; if we see it as the strategy of a rebel archangel, set single-mindedly on the damnation of souls. There is available to us a mythology somewhat less dogmatic, though scarcely less luxuriant, worked out by psychologists with their eye a little more closely on the facts.

We all know the difficulty of proving a universal negative by particular evidence. It seemed clear that there were no black swans, until someone went to Australia and found them there. It is a good rhetorical point to ask, "How do you know that there are no spirits who, like wicked men, have revolted from God? And how do you know that they never poke a finger into our affairs?" We shall be forced to reply that we cannot possibly be certain of either negative. But equally, there may be pink elephants and blue kangaroos on a habitable planet somewhere in the galaxies; who is to deny it? Only we shall not trouble our heads with the possibility, until we have evidence of the fact.

And here we will take leave of the devil, with a last remark. It is sometimes said that if we rationalize Satan out of existence, by the same logic we might reason away our Creator. Nothing could be more false. There is no god of evil on any showing. If Satan exists—if there is a bodiless spirit in revolt against God, and troubling the air of our world—it is a particular fact, like the fact of my next-door neighbor's existence, or the fact of his tendency to turn the radio on when I am trying to sleep. Particular facts are proved by particular evidence. I need not have a next-door neighbor; the apartment might be empty; but is it? Either there is evidence that it is occupied, or there is none. But if the empty apartment exists—if I exist—if anything exists, then God exists. For nothing finite exists without a first creative cause.

It may be objected that the point only holds good in the theology of rational speculation. Such a theology may assure us of God's bare existence; but the assurance would not be a saving truth, unless it were clothed with the flesh and blood of God's self-revelation. We find the revelation in the pages of Scripture, and there at least the theology stands on all fours with the demonology. Well, but does it? The truth of revelation is a saving truth, and to be saved we must embrace the will and person of our savior, not of our oppressor. If God's personality is a myth, the way of salvation is a blind alley. But those who walk up it assure us it is not; they find their way into the mind and heart of God. No one, in being saved, claims to go into the mind and heart of Satan. Salvation would, admittedly, be

no salvation if it saved us from nothing; the evils banished must
be as actual as the blessings bestowed. But we are not called
upon to follow the turns and twists of a strategy employed by
the prince of evil. The sureness of the saving path is unaffected,
if there is no such strategy, and no such prince. Satan may be
an allegory, and the forces of evil remain no less loaded with
eternal death, but for the grace of God.

Whether there are fallen spirits may be open to doubt. We
have not met any. But we can conceive the bare idea, by bor-
rowing from our notion of fallen mankind. Here at least we are
up against facts. An individual person may fall from a state of
grace in which, to all outward evidence, he securely stood. He
was a practicing Christian; he becomes an apostate from faith,
and an egoist in conduct. His new attitudes become second
nature, and determine his character. But the doctrine of the
fall, and of original sin, teaches us that the race itself is fallen,
so that every individual person born into the world starts in a
position somehow analogous to that of a man fallen from grace
by his own fault.

Let us say right out that whereas, with reservations, we
disbelieve in the devil, we believe, also with reservations, in
original sin. We have already remarked, in another connection,
that mentality itself, our rational manhood, is a cultural product. An animal physically capable of speech has learnt the
trick of talking, and passed it on, with embellishments, from
generation to generation. By the time any child becomes master
of himself, and capable of reflective decisions, he has been set
by the society which reared him in certain ways of thought,
and in certain attitudes to life. He can revise some of them,
he cannot be rid of them all; he cannot uproot himself entirely
from the soil in which he has grown.

It is really meaningless to ask whether our inherited attitudes are rather good than bad, or right than wrong. It depends on the standard of comparison; we are better than savages, and worse than angels. Perhaps it is reasonable, in an objective view, to put the accent on the positive. Since our inherited mentality makes us men, and without it we should be beasts, it is a blessing, considered as a whole. But subjectively speaking, decent men identify themselves with the best in them, and Christians with what is in conformity with Christ. Since we reckon such attitudes to be ourselves, we take them for granted, and turn our attention upon what hinders or degrades us. "Wretched man that I am," says Christ's apostle, "who shall deliver me from the body of this death?"

It is quite unrealistic to describe the damaging part of our inheritance as the brute or the savage clinging to us, and not yet shaken off. There are vices of which the primitive, not to say the animal, is incapable. Progress in sophistication is not all progress in virtue; the corruption of the best is the worst, and the villainies of the civilized are the blackest. What is, or should be most repugnant to us in the self we inherit, is the product of an untold number of voluntary acts committed by sinful men.

Since sin is voluntary, it need never, ideally speaking, have been committed; men could have gone right from the start and, in proportion as they acquired the power of rational choice, have used it always well. Thinking along these lines, we may form the fantastic project of drawing a graph, in which the curve of mankind's actual performance is shown as a deviation from the line it would have taken, if instead of being a race of Adams, we had been a race of Christs. The graph cannot be drawn; and little sense can be attached to the question whether it was historically possible there should have been no sin; or to the much more famous question, at what point sin should be reckoned to have begun.

We have an inheritance of false or sinful attitudes and ways of thinking; that is what concerns us. Humanists regard it as a relative evil, because it makes a relative difference; human material is not so good as we should wish it to have been. Christians regard it as an absolute evil, because it makes an absolute difference; it debars us from an effective union with the will of God. But this is not the last word; divine grace, the teaching, the passion, and the resurrection of Christ break the barrier down.

Original sin is not actual sin in us. We do not commit it, we are not guilty of it. It sets our will in a false orientation, out of which many actual sins arise. We are guilty of some of these, but not of others. Bad actions which arise from tendencies and principles we have never been led to question are objectively bad, but subjectively considered they are not guilty. In so far as we know better, but acquiesce in inherited attitudes, we incur guilt.

But the exclusion of original sin from the area of personal responsibility is merely theoretical. In practice we cannot draw the line. I inherited the selfish tendencies of a sinful race, implicit in the very speech I learnt, and impressed by a thousand silent examples. But before I cite this false inheritance to excuse the acts I now thoughtlessly perform, I have to consider how far I am responsible for its continued hold on me, by my failure to correct it on past occasions. Our guilt for the falsity of our attitudes is all one piece, we cannot divide it. We know that our ancestors and ourselves must shoulder the blame between us; we cannot attempt to distribute the weight.

The way in which original sin has been traditionally pre-
sented is tied up with an obsolete view of human nature. The
error of the ancients was the assimilation of reasonable mind
to animal body. Mentality, for them, was a fixed set of capacities
common to the members of the human species, very much as
bodily abilities are. An animal kind tends to keep itself steady;
there is a fundamental dogginess about dogs which tends to
prevail, and bring the individuals out true to type. Accidental
circumstances occasionally obstruct the self-realization of the
species, producing poor specimens and deviations. They are the
exceptions, and the norm continues for the most part to
triumph. So with the human animal, only that man has rational
and spiritual properties which are lacking to brutes. These
properties should tend to come right, too, so that every child
should tend to be born sound in spirit. There might be poor
specimens, but a spiritual twist to the whole species would be a
scandal in nature, and require special explanation. It would be
as though the predicament of the whole race resembled that of
a single family deriving a congenital weakness from a common
ancestor. Or should one say that it was like the condition of a
tribe of animals cut off in a habitat where they were forced,
generation after generation, to dispense with items of diet or
other necessaries required for a balanced life? They could still
live, but they could never live well.

Philosophizing a scriptural fable, we might say that Adam,
by misusing his will, had produced a heritable disease of
choice in all his descendants, a vice in the blood. But again
we might say that he had lost them their natural habitat,
the earthly paradise, and cut them off from supplies of grace,
the proper diet of their souls; so that they could hope for noth-

ing better than a stunted spirituality, until a divine initiative should better their condition.

Such speculations as these were the best that could be offered in comment on the moral facts, so long as you started with your mistaken view of man's rational "nature." If, instead, we talk of man's rational culture, the need for them disappears. There is no need to explain why the individual moral agent starts life with tainted attitudes. His being a mortal agent at all is a cultural effect, and the culture was tainted already.

Once the point has been made clear, the ravages of original sin become a historical question. In one sense of the phrase, we do not know what damage original sin has done us, because we do not know what the position of mankind would now be, if no one had sinned. But it is equally true that we do not know what damage was done us by the collapse of ancient Rome; for we do not know what would be the present posture of affairs if the Fifth Century Empire had digested her barbarians. In another sense, we know what the damage was; the schools closed, the cities ruined, the roads fallen into disuse, the administration barbarized, the economy simplified. And in the same sense we can talk rationally enough about the ravages of sin; what strife and cruelty, lust, pride, sloth, and indifference have done.

In that traditional account of man's fall which we have just criticized, it was logical to measure the damage of his sin, not so much by the position he would have now reached if he had remained sinless, as by the standard of an ideal "nature" from which he had fallen away. Since a fantastic view could easily be taken of man's natural perfection, fantastic statements could be advanced about the results of his fall. It seemed only due to the dignity of a rational creature that he should be physically immortal; that he should command the allegiance and respect of the whole animal creation; that his own animal appetites should be his obedient servants, and never run ahead of his reasonable commands, or need to be called to heel. On such suppositions as these, it must be put in the catalogue of Adam's crimes against his offspring that they die after some seventy years, that snakes bite them or microbes infect them, and that they fall in love before they mean to do it.

We cannot suppose that sin has altered man's physical condition, except in ways that make historical sense. Many physical evils have followed from the careless housing of multitudes in large cities. It may be difficult to say how far mere ignorance of hygiene was to blame, and how far a callous self-seeking on the part of the great employers of labor. If the second factor was a cause, then sin was a cause; and not so much the particular wickedness of individuals, as an attitude towards private gain which had become second nature; and this is "original sin."

It would be easy to multiply examples. But more interesting than physical evils are those misfortunes of the mind which can be traced to the same cause. The supreme misfortune is sin itself; a perverse attitude to God, our neighbor, and our own claims or concerns. But how many other mental ills does it bring in its train! The material anxieties, the personal mortifications, the stings of unsatisfied ambition or of vain remorse—we might follow the moralists of all ages in placarding the self-inflicted wounds of egoism and folly. Unbending morality is, indeed, all too ready to pin the blame upon the sufferers. An understanding and a Christian judgment will revise the verdict. Poor creatures, they are as much the victims of their predecessors as of themselves. The self-punishing attitudes they adopt belong to a mentality which they have sucked in with the air they breathe; belong, in a word, to original sin.

Sin not only creates many unnecessary banes, it sharpens many others which are inevitable. Who can measure the objective degree of any pain? We cannot think it away, it hurts whatever we think of it; yet it seems to hurt as much as we think it does. Uncomplaining patience, religious faith, an interest beyond the horizon of our own sorrows, will make bearable, or even happy a life which with other dispositions feels worse than death. And death itself—sin did not literally introduce it, but how much sin has embittered the sting! This is the best gloss which pious interpretation can put on the punishment of Adam. "In the day thou sinnest, thou shall die"— death would not be death, anyhow to believers, if they loved and trusted God. Adam would have died anyhow; but he would not have died the death—the death which sin has made.

Sin, at least, is ours, if it really is sin. No serious-minded Christian who has reconciled himself with the truth by reconciling himself to God, and has received the divine forgiveness, can doubt in that moment that the sins for which he is forgiven were his own work, or that he could have done better, if he would. Sin is ours; and so to derive evils from the effects of our sin is to charge ourselves, and to exculpate God. And one concern in the minds which have thought out doctrines of original sin has been precisely this, to clear God of responsibility for evils of every sort. He meant the universe to be a paradise for rational creatures. If it has proved otherwise, it has been through the perversity of finite wills, to whom by their very nature a free choice of goods and evils belonged. The theologians who have gone this way have accordingly stretched the effect of man's misdoing as far as imagination would reach, and a little beyond. And if, even so, there were still evils unaccounted for by human guilt, the malice of revolted angels might be called in to cover them.

Such exaggerated theories suffer from a fatal defect, in addition to their sheer improbability. They allow the accusation against God's justice, which they had supposedly silenced, to break out in a new place. God is cleared of responsibility for evils, if they can be seen as the natural consequences of our sins. But if the effects of sin are made to extend beyond any natural consequence we can appreciate, God will be accused of attaching fantastic results to simple actions, by an arbitrary harshness; and in such a fashion, that these results fall on the heads of the innocent no less than of the guilty.

The moral surely is that it is better not to cheat, even when, like Job's comforters, we think we are cheating on behalf of the Almighty. Men cannot be led to approve an arbitrary or unnatural account of the wages of sin. They can be persuaded to accept the order of nature as a system which, the more it is looked into, the more it defies our power to think it otherwise. The world is the natural habitat, not of our bodies only, but of our thoughts. Our lungs can breathe no other air, our minds can move in no other universe. The alterations we can meaningfully propose are only of the sort that we might ourselves be imagined physically to produce; the general lines must lie as they are, or we have no foundation even for our fantasies.

Within this world, so constituted as it is, the scope of our freedom is found. Our voluntary acts, whether virtuous, blameworthy, or indifferent, can only realize natural possibilities, and carry natural consequences. We cannot ask that when we sin, we should sin for ourselves alone; our bad acts, just as much as our good, will have all those effects on others which the order of nature implies. What is true of us is true of all; as others will be our victims, so we are the victims of our progenitors. To understand sin is to understand original sin; the sin behind our birth, which casts its shadow over our life.

The influence of sin is subjectively all-pervasive; the world we know is the world in our mind, and all the colors of the picture are falsified by sinful attitudes. But objectively speaking, the effects of sin are limited by natural law; some of our crying miseries are due to it, others are not. Sin may have built the slums, it did not breed the bacilli. It has made many wars, perhaps all; but droughts and earthquakes, no.

The effect of ancestral sin on innocent descendants would provide a motive for divine compassion, if any were needed. If God's justice would be content to let us suffer the consequences of our own guilt, his pity would surely deliver us from the wrongs of men long dead. Yet the long reach of the dead hand is no different in this respect from the close blow of the living fist. If God pities the victims of ancestral error, he pities no less the victims of contemporary unkindness.

But God pities all, and especially the sinner in his own sin. As sin is all one piece, whether "original" or "actual," so the remedy for sin which God provides is all one remedy. His Christ without and his Spirit within convert the heart from living lies, whosever fault they may be. As for the many harms that sin has done, and built into the fabric of the world, he inspires human hands to correct what human hands have perpetrated. We may do much, though we never overtake the task. And our hopes are not bounded by this present life.

CHAPTER VIII

Griefs and Consolations

St. Thomas quotes from St. Augustine the comfortable sentence that God would not suffer evils to befall in his creation, unless it were that he might bring good things out of them. No Christian mind can refuse the formula; only it allows much width of interpretation. It could be taken to mean that the final good strictly justifies the quantity of evil—that no good so great could be produced by any means less costly in pain, or in other misfortune, than those actually employed. Or it might merely be meant that however great and however useless an excess of evil there is in the means, it is outweighed by the happiness of the end.

St. Augustine's life will serve to illustrate his remark, and the different senses that can be read into it. He had spent (so he tells us) the first half of his days in sinful misery, and in ignorance of God. Nothing worse, while it lasted, could happen to a man; and yet, in retrospect, he found the leading of God's hand in all the wanderings of his steps. For these roundabout paths had brought him to a saving faith. Now according to the first sense above suggested for St. Augustine's dictum, it would have been an absolute disaster if he had been able from the beginning to embrace the religion in which St. Monica reared him. Augustine the innocent could never, on this view, have been so perfect a soul as Augustine the penitent actually proved to be. Whereas on the second view proposed, St. Augustine's youthful errors and godless years could be written off as a total loss; only it would be maintained that the loss was unworthy of consideration when compared with the everlasting gain of sanctity and salvation which succeeded it.

If we had to choose between these alternative doctrines, we would take the second. It is intolerable to assert that the agony of God's creatures, not to say their sin, serves him as a means perfectly calculated to produce ulterior ends. Yet we cannot be wholly satisfied with the other view either. Surely we claim too little for an almighty Wisdom, in saying that he contrives to pull some sort of compensatory result out of evils he is somehow powerless to prevent. Shall we not wish to add that what Providence draws out of any situation good or bad is a unique creation from unique materials? It would be a blasphemy to suggest that St. Augustine's sins, or mine, had been a positive gain to our Creator. Yet I have learnt something from my sins, and the Saint, because he was a saint, how much more from his! Without these lessons, neither of us would be the man he is. We should have learnt other lessons, in themselves more advanced, and in virtue of these lessons, would have been better men. Better men, yes, but different beings. We should have had higher qualities, we should not have had just those qualities which make us what we are. And we are as Omnipotence has fashioned us. If we are to speak of omnipotence, an almighty hand, perhaps, could have made us all angels, yet was pleased to give us the stamp we bear, and therefore, we must suppose, wished to have us so.

With these considerations in mind, let us improve on the formula with which we began. Let us say that God would never have allowed evils to subsist in his creation, were it not that he might find in them the occasion to produce good things unique in kind, and dependent for their unique character on the character of the evils in question. A patriot, wearing away his life in a reactionary prison, is not merely to be told that his sufferings will be compensated by some good in the end. He can be told that the divine will has a unique purpose to achieve through them; that he can himself adhere to this purpose, and co-operate with it, if only by his faithful endurance. Even the sinner fallen from grace by his own fault can be assured that the inexhaustible inventiveness of divine mercy has prepared a unique good to be achieved through his repentance; and this in spite of the fact that he would have had a straighter path to higher good by not sinning at all.

When we said just now that the stricter interpretation of St. Augustine's formula could not be upheld, we were relating it to the particular case, not to the general scheme of things. As to that, we must believe that God has acted in all for the best; how could we possibly think otherwise? It was for the best, therefore, that he made a half-chaos of self-moving, brainless forces to be the bottom and soil of his creation, out of which higher forms should arise. But then a semichaos, if it is to be itself, must be a field of limitless accident; and accident is by definition an uncalculated effect. It may be foreseen, provided against, discounted, or profited by; it cannot be intended or arranged. It would be meaningless to say that God himself planned the detail of a chaos, or of a semi-chaos either, in its chaotic aspect. His infinite contrivance draws some good out of every cross-accident, and, as we have argued, a unique good. But he has not calculated the accident with a view to the resultant good. If he had, it would not be an accident, it would only seem to be one.

In the last chapter, we expressed an inclination to reject a literal belief in the devil. At the same time we admitted that talk about him was an allegorical convention serving many useful purposes; and here before us is a case in point. Satan can be called the author of cross-accidents; and to call him so is at least to deny their direct origin from God. It is to represent them as a sort of rebelliousness in things; as more like the work of a demon overruled by Providence, than the work of an angel employed by him. Scripture sometimes gives sickness or the flaws of our moral nature to Satan. The intention is often, perhaps, to express their negative relation to the will of God; and not merely to assign a cause for troubles seemingly incapable of natural explanation.

If we wish to study the ways of divine Wisdom, or to see in any detail how God brings good out of evil, the first clue to the windings of the maze must be the appointed goal. Nor is it enough to know that the goal aimed at is good in general. Why, there are as many sorts of good as there are forms of existence, and as widely different. Unless we are bold enough to ask what particular good God intends in any case, we dream in vain of understanding his particular providences.

We can always ask; we cannot always answer, or even conjecture; and that is why we have often to acquiesce in a blind faith. Yet sometimes we can conjecture, and sometimes we can have a reasonable assurance. And there is, anyhow, before our

eyes that last and universal end which God has disclosed
and, by disclosing, has conferred on our present state the
highest blessing he could bestow, or we receive.

Indeed, if we are speaking of the ills that are peculiar to man,
we can say nothing of God's purpose in regard to them which
has not some reference to that one ultimate and revealed end.
The old women, nodding their heads and sighing over their
neighbors' misfortunes, offer pious-sounding consolations which
are the merest nature-lore. In so far as they express any truth,
it is a truth belonging to the animal level. "Poor dear Mary, she
died, but it was a happy release; she had suffered so much
pain, and there was no other way out. . . . Poor old John,
crippled with the rheumaticks; but he's more comfortable tied
to his chair than breaking his back at the digging; that garden
of his would have been the death of him. God knows best."
What do these sentiments express, but the general balance of
animal life; the effect of pain in economizing exertion, and of
death in putting an end to pain?

The old wives' reflections tread closer to Christian ground
when they bear on the correction of faults, or the formation
of character. "Don't you know about young Harry? He hurt his
spine and kept his bed eighteen months, just at the age when
boys grow strong and daring. But it all turned out for the best;
it made him so much more thoughtful than other lads. . . . It
was hard luck on Tom, his great plans coming to nothing;
like all these contractors, he was bursting to expand. Only
before his disappointments he was so pleased with himself,
he'd no time for anyone; while now he listens to you quite
civil-like. These trials are sent to teach us."

The other old ladies assent to their gossip's moralities, like a
flock of ducks quacking in chorus. They specialize in being

wise after the event; and in such a field, indeed, there is little other wisdom to be had. No one can be sure beforehand how a man's character will be affected by the trials he undergoes. Tom's business disappointments may not make him gentle, they may make him morose. So Tom, in turn, becomes a trial to his mother and his wife. These women, perhaps, rise to the level of their opportunities and edify the old ladies by an exemplary cheerfulness. But then, again, they may not. The whole family, a prey to ill-temper and mutual irritation, becomes a trial to the neighborhood. It will be admirable if it brings out the best in the neighbors; but very likely it brings out the worst.

The evils of our life have an alarming tendency to spread, and to breed other evils. Every extension of the trouble is a possible occasion of good, through the challenge it throws down to character, or the appeal it makes to kindness. But how far the evil may have run and multiplied, before the appeal is heard, or the challenge taken up! And even where the virtue is forthcoming to meet the opportunity, in how many other directions the evil may be answered with evil! The good Samaritan, by his kindness and resource, broke the barrier of prejudice and made a neighbor of an enemy. The priest and the Levite, passing by on the other side, confirmed themselves in their self-righteous egotism.

The old women like to say that what happened was all for the best. They are probably wrong. Good, even animal good, such as physical health or a moderate plenty, is a more fertile breeder of good on the whole—yes, even of moral good—than distress of any kind can be. Were it otherwise, we should be faced with an intolerable dilemma. We should be bound to fear that in consulting our friends' natural happiness, we should

be imperiling their spiritual salvation. Like certain truly fiend-
ish monastic superiors and novice-masters, we should feel
called upon to arrange artificial mortifications for our juniors,
and to twist the tails of our fellow creatures for the good of
their souls.

Good breeds more good than any evil can. It is a special
revelation of God's divine power that he is able to bring some
good even out of evil. But his use of evil for good ends does
not immediately sterilize it; it continues to breed after its
own kind. What perhaps most offends us in the old women's
talk is a suggestion implied, rather than stated; the suggestion
that the evil they deplore finds its characteristic or dominant
effect in the redeeming feature they fix upon. The boy's motor-
cycle slipped, and he was smashed against the wall. The effect
of the bereavement on his father's heart may have been truly
edifying; from a besotted, possessive parent he changed into
a general philanthropist. But it is almost indecent to mention
the fact; still more, to dwell upon it with any satisfaction.
Who cares about the old man, anyway? He has had his life.
The young man, alas!, was cut off in his prime. His promise
was unfulfilled; he never married the girl who loved him; he
had no posterity. Nothing that happened to his father can
make any difference to so absolute an evil.

Of all consolations the most glib and the most indecent in
the ears of unbelievers is the promise of an invisible and an
eternal good. "The boy was smashed against the wall, his life
ran out in blood and soaked away into the grass; but his
soul is saved and treasured, every drop; all will be poured
back into immortal veins, it will animate the body of his
glory; he will see the face of God, and enjoy a happiness in
comparison with which the best pleasure of his golden youth

was the shadow of a shade." The offence here is not that the compensation is either inadequate or irrelevant, but that it is fantastic and unproved. Anyone can spin phrases about a world hidden from sight, where all journeys end, and from which no traveller returns.

And yet there is no other consolation but this which carries any force. The issue is all or nothing; either we believe, or we do not. The half-believing moralities of the old women fall flat, so long as they equivocate on this single point. Has the boy perished as though he had never been, and is his father to go the same way in a few years? Then how trivial it is that the old man should sublimate his disappointed parenthood in an enthusiasm for the reclamation of young gangsters! He has begun his charitable work somewhat late in life; it is not to be thought that he will make much of a showing at it. But once admit that the characters of the tragedy are immortal souls, and the balance alters. The boy's premature death, though an undoubted flaw in the order of nature, and a wound in the body of human affection, is not so blank a loss as to make the mention of redeeming consequences an indecency; while the opening of the father's narrow heart, being the preparation of a soul for glory and a beginning of heaven on earth, obtains a weight which may fairly tell in the scale of compensations. Even the old man's ill-practiced philanthropy begins to have an incalculable radiation. He may not appear an effective agent in his chosen work, but divine charity once lighted in him will kindle his fellow-workers, or awake a response somewhere. And all charity, visible or invisible to human eyes, is everlasting life.

Yet however believing we may be, we hesitate to offer open consolations, unless we have an equal right to grief. Let the father console the fiancée with immortal hopes, or she him.

The friends of both hold back, for either they do not feel the grief with equal force, or if they think they do, cannot expect to be believed. It may give them some title to speak, if they have a comparable and acknowledged grief of their own; they too have lost lovers or sons. Why should this help? Because it is not a matter of seeing a consequence, it is a matter of feeling grief and hope. You may see that present evil lies in the path to an immeasurably greater good, and yet you may feel present grief with immeasurably greater force than future hope. And it seems no consolation to say that good will one day come. You must be able to say that divine hope can temper human grief. Any Christian can say the first; only a sufferer can venture the second.

It is indeed the common character of grief, as also of pain, to be obsessing; and we ask too much, if we demand that the saving action of God should not only redeem us from sorrow, but should make the redemption to be felt by us in the moment when the sorrow seizes us. But then it is not on feeling that Christians plant their feet, it is on faith; and faith is an act of the will. The Christian sufferer will scarcely lay hold on future hope by an imaginative delight in blessings still unrealized. But he may have a practical belief in the present work of God, through which Providence prepares good things beyond the grasp of our understanding. He may adhere to the divine purpose, and co-operate with it.

It is this practical aspect of faith which makes the riddle of particular providence appear so urgent a question. The Christian sufferer need not know why the blow was struck. He wants to discover what God is doing in face of it, so that he may do it too. He cannot set about directly to alter his feelings. He can only consider what to do with himself, or what to do for his fellow-sufferers, in the destiny which has fallen so heavily upon him. And being a Christian, he will want to do what God is doing.

And yet, as we said above, it is hard to be wise in the tracing of particular providences, except after the event. Looking back over a tract of time, we can see how circumstances have shaped us, even in spite of ourselves, and regret that we have put so many obstacles in the path of a mercy we failed to discern. Yet we probably do ourselves an injustice if we suppose that we could have seen the way plain in front of us. We could only have found it by letting ourselves be led up it. This manner of proceeding is not so mysterious as it sounds. We become sensitive to the leading of God by a faithful attention to common claims, and an obedience to his revealed will. The Christian sufferer goes on quietly with his duties, and embraces his opportunities of well-doing, sustained by the general belief that through these things God will make suffered evils fruitful of good. He needs a faith in the working of particular providence, not a detection of it.

Pain, grief, and every sort of discontent put a drag on action and drain the color out of enterprise. Merely to resist the deadening influence, and go on with life at all, may be an effort almost too great. Half the sufferer's business is to suffer bravely, to endure and not give way. In such a state of being, he will find it the most direct consolation to know that his suffering has itself a place in the redemptive action of God. And this is the gospel of Christ's Passion—that God saves us not only out of suffering, but by suffering. The world is redeemed by the sufferings of Christ; and his sufferings work out their divine effects through the sufferings of Christians.

There is nothing morbid or masochistic about the doctrine

of redemptive suffering. It does not teach that God is pleased with the costly effusion of blood, with the torture of brain or of nerve, rather than with the health and happiness of his creatures. The suffering he approves, and himself undertakes, is redemptive. Redemptive of what? Of evils which are in any case there, and which will not be overcome by our running away from them. It is our faith that in standing against them we can vanquish them, through our union with the heroic and all-conquering Passion of Christ.

But that is not all. Our religion teaches us that suffering is one; our endurance assists the endurance of other men, as theirs assists ours. The suffering endurance of the individual man may not seem to him important; he does not want to think of achieving holiness in his own person, or of acquiring the virtues. He would much rather that a merciful Providence should shorten his painful life. In such a mood it is something for him to be reminded that his endurance supports those in a position to feel it, and through them, others unknown and uncounted. His patience is an unspoken prayer; it will only gain in force if it finds utterance in intercession.

To live is to do; while we have something fruitful to do, we are commonly content. The sufferer finds his action, in the ordinary sense, cramped or enfeebled. The mere supporting of his trouble uses up such energy as he has. He is to learn that this mere supporting is a doing, an action of great power, a co-operation with almighty Love. It was thus the martyrs endured their deaths. They did not see themselves as passive victims of pagan malice. They died willingly, to honor and to implement Christ's victory. They were his soldiers, and they fought a battle they could not lose, except by their own treason. For though they were weak in their own strength, they had the grace of God; and nothing could be stronger than omnipotence.

We speak of martyrdom in the past tense; the tyrannies of our own time have seen the folly of making martyrs. What, indeed, could be more self-defeating than the measures of the old Roman government? To pick the most distinguished, or the most stubborn of the Christians, and do them to death in amphitheatres, before ten thousand eyes, with all the circumstance and drama of a Spanish bullfight—was it surprising that the blood of the martyrs proved to be the seed of the Church? No antichristian regime is likely to repeat the error. Christians will be condemned for fiddling the currency, or leaguing with the national enemy; for economic sabotage or political subversion; not for loyalty to Christ. They will not be given the opportunity of attesting the faith they profess; they will be given the opportunity of confessing the crimes they have not committed; and they will do it; for they will be subjected to a technique of suspended torture and psychological persuasion capable of breaking any mind.

So there are to be no more martyrs, only involuntary apostates; and this depressing fact seems to some of us the greatest obstacle in the way of faith. The Christian's sheet anchor was the promise of God never to fail or to forsake us; and must we not admit that it has given way? We knew well enough that the servant of God would be spared neither pain, sorrow, disappointment, sickness, nor death. But in all these things, we had been taught, God gave us the victory, if we had the will. No one could rob us of our integrity but by our complicity. Above all, no one could cheat us of our loyalty to God. We thought they could not, but now it seems they can. We thought Christ had suffered the worst, but now it seems he did not.

He never came against scientific mind-twisting. By the time he was broken on the cross, he was nailed to his claim. The agony brought him to his cry of abandonment, but the placard hung over his head. His death continued physically to advertise the identity of a crucified man with the king in God's Israel.

No, Christ did not (it is true) suffer under conditions humanly impossible for the achievement of his purpose, or the upholding of the gospel by his death. He suffered all that men can endure; he did not suffer what they cannot. But then his death, like the whole of his life, was providentially ordered with a view to his saving mission. He did not suffer at the hands of enemies who systematically destroyed his intellect before they killed his body. But neither did he die of a lingering disease, which might have had the same effect in corrupting the mind. Contemporary history may have shown us that there is no guarantee in the fidelity of God against martyrs recanting by no fault of their own. We have long had the evidence that there is no guarantee, either, against sufferers blaspheming or apostatizing under the influence of a sickness which attacks their brains.

The promises of God are addressed to open ears and living hearts. They are not addressed to brutes, still less to stocks or stones. We are ourselves incapable of responding to them or putting our trust in them when we are asleep, or stupified, or dead (though God will raise us). Now, we may be half-awake before we are asleep, fall into coma by gradual stages, and die by inches. Somewhere the point will be passed when we are no longer responsive to the promises of God. It is certainly devilish that human torturers should find means to hold their victims just over the point, should bring about an artificial sleepwalk of the soul, and destroy integrity while they preserve speech and action. It is devilish, but the devil loses his game by overacting his part. The victims are not damned when they recant, if, as moral beings, they are no longer there.

In such a case, as in death itself, faith is driven to her last resource. There is another life; God raises the dead. And certainly no servant of God is to lose his everlasting reward because he failed to glorify God when the power to do so had been destroyed in him.

Religious truth has a double aspect. On the one side it gives us an account of things which are so in any case, and whether anyone believes them or not. However many men are atheists, God created them; and their better aspirations are an awareness of his will, though they deny it. They serve his purposes when they go right, and offer occasions for his mercy when they go wrong. They do not understand themselves; but the believer understands them. So much for the factual side of religious truth. The other side is practical. It offers a program of action, through which men are to transcend their miseries, and enter into the saving purposes of God.

Now if we are considering apparent obstacles to any Christian belief, it is essential to decide first which side of this division the belief in question belongs; whether to the program of action, or to the description of fact. The program of action is for the man who can ask, or be brought to ask, "What shall I do to be saved?" It is the answer to his question. It is absurd to complain that the blessing of a true faith is withheld in this life from those who do not look towards God, whether it be by their own fault, or because the capacity has been destroyed in them. Christ preaches salvation to those who have ears for the gospel, much as an agricultural improver offers better methods for cultivators able to understand and willing to try. We may be sorry, but we can scarcely be outraged, if those who do not take up the methods go without the improved results.

But the man who falls outside the sphere of practical truth remains in the sphere of the factual kind. God does not cease to be his God because the man forgets him. He cannot consciously co-operate in his own salvation, but God can bring it to pass. He cannot directly assist the salvation of others, but God will use other agents. Faith is not a program for him; but the faith of those who have faith is faith in a program which embraces him, for it embraces all things.

We are all of us well aware that men may be excluded in this life from the sphere of practical truth, that is to say, of faith, by no fault of their own. But we should like to deny, if we could, that anyone once in it falls out of it, unless it be by his own fault. It is distressing to admit that the action of disease, or the cunning of torture, can abolish a Christian, while the man he was, and is no longer, continues to live and move among us. The abolition may be temporary, or it may, for this world, be permanent. If it is temporary, the man recovers; if it is permanent, the best thing has died in him while he lives, and until God raises the dead.

Why is it, though, that brainwashing and the breaking of martyrs by technique raise so peculiar a stumbling block to faith? Heaven knows, they constitute an appalling outrage on humanity. They show that human beings are capable of diabolic disregard for one another's person. But there is no novelty here; we have always known as much. There is nothing men will not do to one another under the pressure of supposed necessities. I remember discussing the rules and conventions of civilized warfare with a friend in 1939. "It's no use talking," he said. "We shall stick at nothing. There's nothing too bad to be true in war. When we think we've reached the moral bottom, another depth will open, and down we'll go." Martyr-breaking techniques are certainly bad; but not uniquely so, when compared, let us say, with the bombing of Hiroshima.

The peculiar shock to faith is not, then, that anything so frightful should be done by some men, and suffered by others, or that God should allow it. What troubles us so strangely is the disturbance of our attitude to our own possible future. "Whatever happens," we have been used to think, "I shall hold on by the grace of God; or if not, I shall have myself to blame." Now it seems we can say nothing of the sort.

It is the theme of the chapter we are writing, that God brings good out of the blackest evil. It is time we asked ourselves what good he may bring out of coldhearted contrivances designed to make tyranny martyr-proof. Different men might hazard different answers, and they might all be right. The purposes of God are more many-sided than we shall be able to think them, when we have all laid our heads together. So among other answers, the following might hold a place. These monstrous inventions have pressed home the distinction between Christian faith and Stoic confidence. When we said that we would never lose our Christian integrity except by our own fault, we told ourselves that the ground of our trust was the omnipotent grace of God. But perhaps we took grace for granted, and were confident that we, splendid creatures, had it in us to respond to grace, if it came to a showdown.

The traditional picture of the martyr as a Christian athlete, in perfect training for the spiritual combat, owes something to the Stoic morale of self-sufficiency, however tempered by more Christian attitudes. But now pride goes by the board. We have no assurance of being able to escape the last apparent infamy. We must rely on the mercy of God, who raises both shame and glory from the dust of death.

In the course of our discussion, we have used a black-and-white distinction between two classes of men. There are those for whom religion is a practical truth, believed in and obeyed, and there are those about whom it is still a factual truth, though they neither obey nor believe. The first sort get their feet on to the path which leads out of the world's evils to an everlasting good; the second sort wait until another life for their redemption.

The distinction is oversimplified, that goes without saying. But if it is to have any validity at all, one point must be made clear. The path which faith finds, and unbelief misses, may be the only path to everlasting good; it is not the only path out of common miseries which can promise immediate relief. The art of happiness is often well understood by unbelievers. They may not have the Sermon on the Mount, but they have the Ethics of Aristotle, or more probably the maxims of their grandfathers and uncles. They know that pain, sorrow, and personal disappointment can be kept within bounds by turning one's attention to the day's work, and interesting oneself in the joys or griefs of friends. They know that most anxiety is needless folly, and that by limiting our concern to matters requiring our decision, we can economize our fears. They know that the wise man will curb his hopes, to lessen his regrets; and lower his demands, to lighten his resentments. They know that pleasure is not found by seeking it, and that contentment is the fruit of activity. There are evils, admittedly, about which nothing can be done: above all, death. But where there is nothing to be done, there is nothing to be thought of, either; the man of sense disciplines his imagination, and keeps it from dwelling long on sorrows he cannot mend.

Sometimes, observing the practical folly of the spiritual-minded, we could wish that they would shut up the Sermon on the Mount, and open the Proverbs of Solomon. They have the highest happiness, no doubt; but why should they not have the lower happiness, too? People may show heroic charity in an awkward marriage; but suppose that a little common sense would make it a comfortable one? Common sense, indeed, needs to be sanctified; but it is an unreal sanctity which does not clothe itself with common sense.

Unbelief approaches the spirit of religion in various degrees. Where faith bears the evils of existence, by co-operating with a Providence which draws good out of them, humane idealism breaks the obsession of personal sorrow, by identifying itself with the forward march of mankind. Cannot a man forget his selfish regrets, in serving and contemplating the advance of the Race? Though we die before we see the result, we can die knowing that we have forwarded a glorious consummation.

Can we, though? Suppose history reverses Eliot's line, and the world ends, not with a whimpering, but with a banger— and the bangers are already in production. It may be melodramatic to imagine a suicide of mankind; an extermination of Chinamen at least is hardly to be thought of. But the disaster may still be such as to put a dead end to anything you or I might hope to have promoted. Despairing of personal immortality, men take refuge in the open future of their civilization. With one tug at the cord Death draws the curtains on history, and laughs. There is no getting round death. We have to go through it; all we can hope for is resurrection.

It is sometimes supposed that a disaster to our culture

would be a defeat for Providence, or rather, a disproof of it. So readily does Christianity slip back into the place of that old political religion which hallowed the existing order and deified kings. If Jerusalem fell, God's cause would be lost. On the contrary, said the prophets to their people; nothing but the fall of your ramparts will cure you of trusting in lies. When your world is in ruins about you, there is hope of your walking humbly with your God. The first Christian generations went further in their detachment. They knew well enough that they were outside the walls, whether of Jerusalem or of the Roman Babylon. They waited calmly for the collapse of the city, together with the culture it stood for. Corruption had eaten too deep into the system for it to be redeemed or purified; and God would be visibly justified in its destruction, when Antichrist was crowned. Idolatrous perversity would be enthroned in the government, and acclaimed by willing subjects. When the fire of God fell, it would fall on self-confessed iniquity. The deluge of flame would not be the beginning of history, it would be the end. What followed would be nothing earthly, but the resurrection of the dead.

We cannot exactly endorse the expectation of those first Christians, since subsequent fact refuted it. But if those men could be Christians, and think as they did, it can be no true or inseparable part of our Christianity, to think the opposite. We are not obliged to be disciples of Constantine, who gilded the pagan empire with a Christian halo. For a millennium and a half, wheat and tares have grown together. Which of us can be sure that it is not now in the designs of Providence to have a day of harvest, and bring the long-tolerated mixture to an end?

Suppose the extreme; suppose the extinction of the race.

If heaven and not utopia is the goal, why should we assume that God must be discontented with a finite number of heavenly citizens? Why think that he must desire to recruit more souls forever, and therefore need history without end, in which to recruit them? Or if he does mean to have more talking animals, has he not all the ages, and all the galaxies, in which to find them? Who knows, indeed, whether in this present time he has not already a hundred colonies of rational creatures, tucked away in the vast folds of space?

Scientists talk now quite soberly of voyaging among the stars, and landing on other planets. It is not for a layman in their art to contradict them. But he cannot help foreseeing that a principle of diminishing returns for increased effort will make itself felt in their area of enterprise. With immense contrivance and disproportionate cost, you may get a few human bodies alive on to the moon. They will not be able to walk at liberty in those argent fields; they will plod round with weighted feet in glass-contained bubbles of artificial atmosphere. Like the most inadaptable of earthly colonists, they will make it their whole endeavor to gather round them a poor and expensive imitation of their life at home. They will see some strange sights through the windows; and in their few moments of leisure from the urgent business of keeping alive, they will record on their instruments registrations of undoubted value to science.

Those of us who sit in our armchairs, and send our thoughts where bolder spirits hope to set their feet, have a somewhat similar experience. It seems that we cannot do justice to the purposes of God, or balance the arithmetic of good and evil, without mapping the universe, and running our heads against the end of history. And yet the further we go beyond the range of our natural sympathies, the less light we can see. It is no occasion, really, for surprise. Our inquiry is of good and evil; and these are qualities (if we may call them such) revealed to us by the motion of our heart. Evil is what, after all consideration, it detests, and good, what it embraces. Now the heart speaks readily and warmly where it is at home. The coldness of the outer spaces chills it into silence.

There will always be two extremes, between which philosophical reflection will oscillate. There will be the scientific, and there will be the humane philosophers. The first sect will point to the folly of judging the universe from man; the second will contend that such folly is our only wisdom, because man is all we know at first hand; of the rest we have nothing but diagrams. The two contentions are, of course, not really at variance; each represents a side of the truth, and each is justified in its own sphere. But if we are talking of good and evil, we fall within the sphere of the humane philosophy. Good and evil are known by the heart; and the heart does not act outside the range of human affections.

Every one of us is bound to take the little world his heart contains as his example of the incidence of banes and blessings, or of God's providence in allowing and in curing harms. And if he seeks light on his own little world by looking outside it, it is into other little worlds that he looks, not into diagrammatic perspectives of human history, let alone of cosmic structure. Reading at large in the Bible, I come upon the story of King David, written for us by an author the best part of three thousand years old, who had the art to make his characters live, and to create for us all the relationships of a small Oriental court. The joys and sorrows, the hopes and fears of the group, with the pattern of their destinies, enter into direct connection with the balance of our present experiences. If it were not so, the picture would not live for us, or stir our sympathies as it does. I turn to another part of Scripture, and find in the Gospel history that little world which holds the best key to the meaning of all our little worlds.

Goods and evils, then, are known where the shoe pinches, or where the heart dilates. In like manner God's creatorship is perceived when we ourselves are the beings created, and dependent on his will; or if not ourselves, then neighbors who concern us; and others only afterwards, and by analogy. Since I do not know except in the remotest way what it is like to be a snail, or an oak tree, and not at all what sort of existence a molecule of iron enjoys or exercises, how can I think what it is for any of these to have their being from God? Whether we choose it or not, we must stand to ourselves as our sample of creaturehood, just as we must stand to ourselves for our sample of a being that is subject to good and evil. Indeed, experience of creaturehood and experience of value are intimately linked; our sense of God is dependent on our sense for evil and good. God is felt as the source of good; or, if you say he is felt as the source of existence, you must acknowledge that the existence which is known as something bestowed by God has a positive character; it is itself a blessing, and enriched with blessings. In this fact lay the root of Job's agony. He had known God as the author of blessing, and the blessing had turned to a curse. Where, then, was God?

The same issue faces Christian sufferers, though their resources for meeting it are infinitely greater than Job's were. Associating themselves with the sufferings of Christ, they find the soul of good in the heart of evil. They identify themselves with the will of a God who raises the dead.

The inquiring mind is not to be turned back from its chosen path. Speculative questions deserve speculative answers; and so in this book we have tried to satisfy those whom the riddle of providence and evil intrigues or torments. But the value of speculative answers, however judicious, is limited. They clear the way for an apprehension of truth, which speculation alone is powerless to reach. Peasants and housekeepers find what philosophers seek in vain; the substance of truth is grasped not by argument, but by faith. The leading of God through evil out of evil and into a promised good is acknowledged by those who trust in his mercy. The balance of the world is good to them, though in the eyes of onlookers their misfortunes go beyond endurance. I remember the happiest man in a hospital, lying broken-backed forever in pain on a water bed, overflowing with gratitude to those who tended and those who visited him, and blessing us all by his prayers.

There are those whom the sight of unassisted misery in others chiefly appalls, and leads them to curse or to deny the Author of the Universe. They are seldom those who yield to the natural pressure of sorrowful scenes on a compassionate heart, and give themselves to the work of relief. An overmastering sense of human ills can be taken as the world's invitation to deny her Maker, or it may be taken as God's invitation to succor his world. Which is it to be? Those who take the practical alternative become more closely and more widely acquainted with misery than the onlookers; but they feel the grain of existence, and the movement of the purposes of God. They do not argue, they love; and what is loved is always known as good. The more we love, the more we feel the evils besetting or corrupting the object of our love. But the more we feel the force of the besetting harms, the more certain we are of the value residing in what they attack; and in resisting them are identified with the action of God, whose mercy is over all flesh.

Imperfect Lives

One of the commonly reckoned evils of human life is the death of speechless infants, before they reach the stature of humanity; another is the survival of imbeciles, who are incapable of ever attaining it.

Both these misfortunes evidently belong to the animal order. It is an accident common to organic existence that weak, puny, and imperfect examples of any given species should sometimes be produced. It is a problem for medicine, not for theology. In fact, infant mortality has been enormously diminished by science; we have had less success so far with defective brains.

The theological problem specially posed by these disorders is not that they should be permitted to befall our kind, but that we do not know how we should relate to the mercy of God beings who never enjoy a glimmer of reason. Are they capable of eternal salvation, or are they not? Out of natural piety, and a respect for the divine image in man, we treat them as human. We do not kill our imbeciles; we baptize dying infants, and give them Christian burial. We are inclined to think of a rational person walled up, as it were, in their bodies, and bricked in with stupid flesh; he is cruelly treated in being denied light, air, and utterance. This, at least, is a fallacy of sentiment; the rational person is not there. And if it is an amiable absurdity in us to pity his non-existence, we should not suppose him to be the object of an all-wise Compassion.

Newly born infants are irresistibly appealing to their mothers, and to all who share the parental attitude. But then so are newborn kittens to cats. Perhaps the great evil of infant mortality is parental disappointment. The grief may be as sharp as any, but scarcely as lasting. We do not sorrow in after years for children who have scarcely lived, as we do for hopeful boys and girls cut off in the midst of their growth. Children who attain no use of speech or reason at all remain to grieve our eyes; but it is not like having a clever child made imbecile by accident or sickness.

If there ever was a speaking and loving person, there is a creature for God to immortalize. It is nothing to God that he died lacking the use of reason; or what are we to say of those who die in their sleep? But if the reasoning person never developed, what are we to think? The baby smiled before it died. Will God bestow immortality on a smile? Shall we say that every human birth, however imperfect, is the germ of a personality, and that God will give it an eternal future? We shall still have to ask why the fact of being born should be allowed a decisive importance; we shall wonder what to think of children dying in the womb, or suffering abortion; and we shall be at a loss where to draw the line. Not that it will be any easier to draw it if we equate the origin of an immortal soul with the attainment of speech or reason. For we shall still have to ask, What degree of reason? Rationality comes by stages in those who acquire it, and not all imbeciles are totally mindless.

We do not know where to draw the line; that is to say, we do not know where God draws it. But we may be sure that he loves and saves whatever is there to be saved or loved; if his love or power does not act, it is because there is nothing for it to act upon. He makes no arbitrary discrimination. Even if he had to discriminate, he would do it, rather than suspend the designs of his mercy towards the human race. We shall scarcely attribute to God the mentality of a government clerk, who would rather distribute no benefits at all, than lack a clear rule of thumb by which to assign them.

What we have written is, we know, quite useless to those who rear imbeciles or lose infants, and wish to relate the offspring of their bodies to the mercy of their Creator. But there is no certain light on this painful matter; nor is there any honesty in dogmatizing where we have nothing to go upon.